# BAD JOBS & BULLSHIT

# BAD JOBS & BULLSHIT

# IT'S UNLIKELY THAT WE'LL BE MISSED

Brad King (Ed.), Amber Peckham (Ed.), Jessica Dyer (Ed.)

The Geeky Press

Indianapolis

# Contents

# Special Thanks

*"Socks on fire"*

Susan Yount's poem "Socks on fire" appears in the anthology *Eating Her Wedding Dress: A Collection of Clothing Poems* published by Ragged Sky Press in 2009.

*"I worked for a boss who wanted sex"*

Susan Yount's poem "I worked for a boss who wanted sex" was previously published in *Jet Fuel Review*.

*"Me and Another Girl Work Second Shift at Motto Mart Gas Station"*

Susan Yount's poem "Me and Another Girl Work Second Shift at Motto Mart Gas Station" was previously published in *Glint Literary Journal*.

*Part I Photo*

Photo by Toms Baugis under the Creative Commons license. Use of this image does not serve as an endorsement of this project by the creator. Image was altered. Original image: https://flic.kr/p/4PBHNM

*Part II Photo*

Photo by Alexander Baxevanis under the Creative Commons license. Use of this image does not serve as an endorsement of this project by the creator. Image was altered. Original image: https://flic.kr/p/HKhvNV

*Part III Photo*

Photo by Pilar Berguido under the Creative Commons license. Use of this image does not serve as an endorsement of this project by the creator. Image was altered. Original image: https://flic.kr/p/8kkGSH

# Introduction

## By Amber Peckham

Life is a whole lot of bullshit, period. This book will not change your mind about that. It won't empower you, and it probably won't teach you any life lessons. Our only aim is that is amuse you, and even that is a crapshoot.

Your group of intrepid editors– Brad King and Amber Peckham of The Geeky Press, and Jessica Dyer of Vouched Books—realized one day over coffee that instead of resisting the constant stream of bullshit in the literary world, we could harness it and do some pretty cool things. After all, all writers are liars. There couldn't be much harm in us just trying to play pretend that we were going to publish a book. We decided to fake some authority and see how people responded. We put out the call for submissions for this anthology via a Google search for college writing programs (thanks, AWP) and by nagging the shit out of our friends (none of whom ended up in here, incidentally).

We have no clout whatsoever—we don't work for a publishing house, we're not hiding a printing press in a basement, and we aren't part of whatever mythical body of old white men drinking scotch in a shadowed library determines the literary canon. We're just people who have worked a lot of bad jobs, and put up with a lot of bullshit, and decided we wanted to hear about how that same phenomenon happened to others.

If you're reading this, and continue reading, it's because you want to hear about that too. We think you'll find the mix of essays, short stories, and poems in this collection speak to common experiences and make you feel less alone in your struggle against the grinding machine of entropy. If not, well, then, sorry, all we've done is heap more bullshit onto your already full, stinking, awful plate. Maybe you should do your own Google search and make your own book.

We don't say that with insincerity or snarkiness– really, it's just as easy as harnessing the bullshit instead of being buried by it. Frustrations and disappointment may be part of the human condition, but that doesn't mean we have to lay down, roll over, and expose our underbelly to the horrors of mundanity. Our contributors, each in their own way, resisted that call. And luckily, they answered ours.

# PART I

# Fiction

*Edited by Amber Peckham*

# 1

# The Racist is Always Right

### By Alyssa Hubbard

I worked at a large chain department store in the southeast. We specialized in everything outdoors, from guns to swim trunks, which catered well to the caveman-like conspiracy theorists and government haters alike. He was an elderly man named Eddy. As a self-proclaimed Christian, I found it strange that he was always roaming the marine aisle on Sundays, rather than the church pews.

The first Sunday I met him, I opened the store. As soon as the store opened, Eddy was there. He made a beeline for the counter gripping something in his hands.

I smiled.

"Hello, how are you?"

He stared at me, grunting. His overalls hung off the sides of his naked shoulders, revealing a patch of white, curly hair in the center of his chest. Dirt and grease hung in the wrinkles of his face and arms. It was hard to tell if he was tan or if it was just a layer of dirt. His receding hairline formed a crescent moon on the top of his head, leaving a wall of white and black tuft surrounding it. Had he not been frowning, he might have looked like my own grandfather.
"You know why I don't go to church anymore?"

He dropped a broken reel on my counter before pushing a full pinch of chew into his front lip. I eyed the return suspiciously. We didn't carry that reel anymore. He'd probably had it for years. Still, our 'no hassle' return policy kept me from saying so.

"Is this a return, sir?"

Without answering, he dug into the front pocket of his overalls and pulled out a crumpled mess that might have once been a receipt, but had been used as a napkin. He dropped it on the counter as I held out my hand to take it from him. I stared at the counter, then looked at my still outstretched hand. I met his gaze and he was still idly chewing, just staring at me.

"Too many damn Mexicans."

My stomach condensed to the size of a walnut. I could feel my breakfast hot in my throat. The taste of blended eggs and bile made me gag as I plucked the receipt from the counter, doing my best to smooth it out and avoid the unidentifiable stains. I began typing it into my register.

"And don't get me started on the blacks."

There was a whistle, and out of the corner of my eye I could see him spitting a putrid, oily liquid into a soda bottle. I could taste the bacon now burning in my esophagus. My hands shook as I continued to type. My face, of its own accord, was stiffening and tightening into a hard, fearful mask. It was as painful as the one-sided conversation Eddy carried with himself. He didn't seem to notice, and his voice grew louder with his own rising anger. He might not have been at church every Sunday, but he knew how to preach.

"Lazy. Pure laziness. Like the Chinese."

He picked up the dirt-encrusted reel before dropping it back on the counter.

"Can't even get a decent reel by those bastards. This wouldn't be a problem if it was American-made."

He made a show out of pointing and jeering at the 'Made in China' insignia on the reel's handle. One could barely make it out through the red mud caked onto the mechanism. Another whistle, then a grunt. The smell of tobacco and grease hung in the air. My hands just wouldn't move fast enough.

"Damn, are you gonna be done today?"

I swallowed down the ever-rising bile and breakfast, and my voice climbed from my lungs as a shriveled whisper.

"I'm sorry, sir. I appreciate your patience."

Eddy slammed his plastic bottle onto my counter and all progress halted. The only thing still moving was Eddy's bottom lip, which worked and chewed, allowing for a single line of tar to slip down his chin and fall onto my counter.

"I ain't got no patience."

My pulse thrummed wildly in my ears and the corners of my eyes were burning with hot, liquid fear. Eddy groaned, picking up his dirty reel, which left its own pile of dirt and mess amongst the spilled spittle and oil. He then reached across my register and snatched up his receipt.

"Damn it to hell. Even the whites are useless now. Damn bitches don't need to work here if they can't return a damn reel without whining."

All the while, I watched, gaping at him. He walked toward the exit and, instinctively, I called after him.

"Have a nice day."

He looked back long enough to flip me the bird, then continued on his way through the sliding doors. A whine crawled out of my lungs just as the next customer came forward.

I did my best to smile, though it took much more effort than it should have.

"Hello, how are you?"

The woman waddled forward, leaving a trail of unwanted clothing along the product shelving leading up to my register. She smiled with a glazed look in her eye. With her hair still up in curlers and her attire, a t-shirt with a hole exposing her belly button and pants with frosted, pink donuts on them, it was easy to assume she had rolled out of bed and immediately came here to start her day.

Then, her glazed eyes fell onto my counter.

Her lips curled back, then twisted into a bow, and she held her clothes close to her chest as a mother would to a child.

"Disgusting. This is not how a lady – or a faithful employee, for that matter –

should treat their customers. What have you done so early in the morning? Do you not clean every night?"

I tried to explain Eddy. Surely if she knew about Eddy, she would be more understanding. It was all in vain as her cloudy eyes cleared to a hard, icy stare.

"I refuse to support such an establishment."

With that, she dropped her brand new, unpurchased, brand name items into the spittle and the dirt on my counter. She then 'humphed' and waddled out of the store.

I didn't even try to wish her a good day.

I stared at the mound of cloth, chewed tobacco, and dirt, unsure of how to proceed. Another woman waddled up to the counter and joined me in my assessment of the pile as she clutched her own purchases to her chest.

"Are you open?"

I stood there for a few moments, contemplating that very question myself. Another woman sidled up next to the first. Then there was another fellow with a receipt and a dirt encrusted fishing rod who lined up behind her. Another woman with three kids came up at the rear of the line, barking into a cell phone. Either she was screaming at the person on the phone or she was threatening one of the children who had begun to climb up the product shelves.

I eyed my line, the pile on my counter, and finally the clock on my register. I opened the store a mere thirty minutes ago. I grumbled an uncommitted yes before scraping the pile off my counter and onto my feet. Tobacco stained my sleeve and was now running onto my shoes. It was still more tolerable than the people who seemed to endlessly filter up to my counter only to comment on the unprofessional state of my work environment. All the while, children were knocking down shelves, men and women alike were trailing clothes and other product around the store, and one man was notably spitting tobacco onto the floor rather than into a bottle or trash can. Yet, the endless complaints were targeted at me. I had only thirty minutes into my shift done. I still had eight hours to go.

# 2

# The Quitter is Illuminated

### By Carlo Matos

A loud fart refracts around the room, so loud that if I didn't know exactly where it was coming from, it would have been difficult to triangulate its origin. This happens so often my students don't even snicker anymore. No one looks up. They keep writing as if it were some kind of foreign cultural practice we have come to accept though it seemed odd at first. We are lucky it is only one. Sometimes it's a whole assonant string, a one hundred foot long deep-sea siphonophore rumbling along the ocean floor. There is no pedagogy class you can take or graduate-level text you can read to address this particular problem. I know because I've looked. It comes from the same spot, the same desk, the same student, who, of course, never misses a day of class.

"Dolores, would you like to work in the hallway?" This has been my only successful gambit. I have a desk permanently reserved in the hallway for her, for Dolores of the Sorrows. She likes to complain the other students distract her and that she can't concentrate, which, of course, is the darkest kind of irony since she's been holding us hostage with her distractions all semester. *Bel Canto* it isn't. Ten years of teaching, ten years of never having a serious problem with behavior, ten years of coming up with creative solutions to help students from less-than-supportive socio-economic backgrounds, students who live in crime-infested parts of the city, students who have children and work several jobs, international students who have escaped some horrible atrocity, and Dolores counters all my moves with ease, with a prodigious ability worthy of Gary Kasparov or his digital nemesis, Deep Blue. I've sacrificed all my most powerful pieces and she has decimated them all but one. If she attacks, I will have little material to defend myself with. Mate is imminent. Had this been chess, I would have long since extended my hand to concede the match, but as it is, I will have to play until there is no escape or the clock runs out.

Dolores, Our Lady of the Sadness—the name says it all, as they so often have in my life. When I first started teaching at this college, I had an amazing Congolese student named Lovemore, which I would come to find out was pronounced, Love-a-more. Actually, his name was Lovemore Dick. Lovemore Dick! Right there in black and white. When I looked at my list of names on the first day of class, I thought my colleagues were having some fun with me. It was a pretty lame joke, but at least they were aware of my existence, which was novel. Adjuncts, for the most part, are basically ignored, though we teach the majority of the students at the postsecondary level. Seventy-five percent of all classes are taught by a giant and largely invisible class of part-time labor, so I thought any place where full-timers would take the time to perpetrate such a ruse, even such a bad one, was probably a good place to be. As I was about to skip over the name, however, some part of me wondered if it were possible for there to be an individual with such an unfortunate name. My curiosity got the better of me, and since there's nothing a student hates more on the first day than to be the one the teacher somehow skips over, I decided to call out the name anyway. My solution was simple; I called only the first name. When no one responded, I knew for certain that it was a joke. It should be pretty easy to discover the culprit, I thought. The first full-time faculty member to ask how my class went would be the traitor—the old *Godfather* routine. Never be the one to set up the meeting. They'll have to get up much earlier in the morning to fool me, or so I told myself.

However, since I had to rush to catch a train to another college in time for my next class, I didn't get the opportunity to discover the identity of my would-be tormentor. And when the class met again, I skipped over the name because I was completely certain this student did not exist. When I was done taking attendance, however, a hand shot up, and, of course, it was Lovemore Dick. He was real. I couldn't believe it. And boy did he live up to his first name. He sat in the front row, raised his hand often but not so much that it became annoying. His writing was not good but he never got discouraged no matter what the grade and was always willing to put in a serious effort. And he had a radiant smile, which was so refreshing in comparison to the dull grimaces of American students.

Around midterm, Lovemore came to visit me in my office. He looked so grim and serious I was afraid he was coming to tell me he was dropping my class. I have lost many great students because their out-of-class lives get in the way of their studies, something the people who are supposed to be measuring "success" can't seem to take into account even though they know better.

"Professor, I'm sure you've noticed that sometimes I don't seem to be paying attention." I hadn't, of course, but I had realized years ago that my students depend on the fiction that I am all-seeing and all-knowing. They take it on faith that I spend every waking moment thinking about them, and the disappointment is profound when it becomes clear that I am not. If I forget a handout I promised, if I blank on a name, if I can't remember off the top of my head every comment I made on a paper, the illusion melts and they have to go back to a reality where no one is thinking about them very much at all. I missed much of what Lovemore was saying but I tuned back in time to hear, "Sometimes, I have hard days." I assured him that it was totally OK. He didn't need to be 100% all the time.

"It's not that," he said. "I have PTSD. I wanted you to know because I love your class and I don't want you to think less of me." I didn't know what to say next. I sensed he wanted to tell me more, but I didn't know how to give him permission.

"Were you a soldier?" Many of my students are current or former military.

"No, but when I was living in Africa, a bunch of soldiers broke into our house and butchered my family." I didn't know what to say so I sat there with my mouth open playing see no evil, hear no evil, speak no evil.

"I was hiding in the bathroom and they didn't see me." He went on to describe how he watched them murder his mother, father, siblings, and grandparents. They shot his father in the head and then went at the others with machetes. He saw the whole thing happen. After they left, he had to wait for hours in the house with his dead family until he was sure they were gone. When night came, he had to step over their bodies in order to get away. Eventually, he said, he made it to Virunga National Park where many other refugees had been living. If only this was as rare a story as it should be, but I've known many students, foreign and domestic, who have had experiences as gruesome as this one. These stories make me wonder if anything I am supposed to teach them could ever make up for such horror.

The hard truth is he barely passed my class. I didn't know what kind of opportunities there would be for him. He was already a cab driver, a doorman, and who knows what else, all while going to school. The deck wasn't stacked against him; it was more appropriate to say he wasn't holding any cards at all. It took this much effort just to get a seat at the card table, and the other players were strapped and quick on the draw. But a year later he was back with me in my transfer-level composition course. This doesn't mean I am a good instructor, by the way. Many students will keep taking the same teacher whether they like them or not. It's the old, devil you know routine. But I, of course, was very happy to have him back. There was one problem, however—his papers were suddenly really, really good. I admit I thought he might be cheating. I wanted to believe those were his papers. If the world owed one person, it was him, and I thought my silly moral conundrum beneath contempt. At least, I wanted to feel that way.

I didn't know if that much improvement was possible in such a short time. I am not that good a teacher, and there was only one course between the first class he took with me and this one. But since there was no real way to be sure, I wasn't going to run the risk of alienating him forever by accusing him, so I graded the papers all semester as if he had written them. The real test would come when my students did their in-class essays at the end of the semester. There was no way to fake the in-class essay, no way to have someone else write it for you, no way to purchase one online—no easy way, anyway. When I got to his paper, I was literally sweating. I kept picking it up and putting it back down. I considered accidentally losing the folder. If the quality of the work was not in keeping with the other essays, I would have to accuse one of my favorite students of all time of cheating. I think I would have rather quit my job. I considered that option too.

When I finally read his essay, I nearly wept. It was so good. Not only was he not cheating, he had actually, truly grown as a writer. It was real. The miracle of Lovemore remained untarnished, unsullied, and unwavering. A few years later, he came to visit campus to tell me he had gotten his Master's degree and was currently pursuing a Ph.D. in psychology. Students like Lovemore are the only reason to keep doing this job. Without him, the scales would have crashed years ago.

"Dolores, would you like to go into the hall?" She says no. Dolores is schizophrenic. She can't help that she's been terrorizing the class on a bi-weekly basis. My students, to their everlasting credit, have been patient, but rifts are starting to appear and I know it won't take much to bring it all crashing down, and when the Nothing sweeps in the darkness will be complete. Community colleges have open enrollment, which I totally believe in, but many of these institutions lack the proper services to support a student like Dolores. It was made clear to me that I would be on my own with her. At least she was mostly quiet when we were writing. Last week during a discussion, Dolores kept interrupting—and, of course, her comments were very rarely on topic. We were pretty accustomed to this too, but she seemed more agitated than normal this day and one of my other students—an older woman named Barbara who was returning to school for the first time in a decade—must have been having a bad day too because she uncharacteristically confronted Dolores. Confronting Dolores is like waging a flame war on Internet trolls. It's a losing battle because they have nothing at stake. Dolores, of course, lashed back and it looked like things were going to unravel, but I managed to intervene and quiet them down. The blow-up seemed to purge Dolores's desire to interrupt that day, but there has been lasting tension between those two since.

A burp from Dolores this time. Any noise or movement that comes from that side of the class makes me so tense my shoulders are starting to pinch towards my sternum, like the dipoles of a horseshoe magnet without the luck. Dolores's hand goes up. As usual, she does not wait for me to call on her.

"What are we doing?" Twenty-five minutes have gone by and now she asks what we're doing. I don't know what keeps my voice steady because this isn't the first time she's done this either. Look into the teacher's eyes. This is where you will see the quit if it is going to happen. The class is over in a couple of minutes so I tell her I will explain it to her after class. I admit I add the word "again" at the end of my statement. I can't help it. I don't have a lot of time between classes, but it's better than trying to deal with her while class is still in session. When class ends, Barbara—Dolores's rival—comes to my desk to ask a question about her paper when out of nowhere, Dolores hip checks her and sends her crashing into the first row of desks. She goes clattering to a knee, which makes a terrible crunching noise when it hits the floor.

For a moment, no one seems to know what to do, but Barbara recovers before I do, and she is up like she knows how to handle herself in a fight. And I have no doubt that she does. Barbara is someone you would describe as no nonsense. Some part of me wants to watch her pummel Dolores into a paste for the trauma she has caused me, but I don't want to be responsible for a fight. Without being conscious of it, I somehow manage to wedge myself between them as they scream at each other. Thankfully no one throws a punch, which is lucky for me because they would have hit me right in the face. I recover enough of my faculties to send Dolores away and tell Barbara to wait until she is gone. Barbara and I go to see the Dean of Student Services who seems very supportive, and for a moment I am sure she is going to remove Dolores from my class, but ultimately she does not. If an outright assault isn't enough to constitute removal, what on earth is? I ask Barbara to sit as far as possible from Dolores and I apologize, like it is my fault, for the fact that nothing is done.

The semester manages, against all expectations, to finally come to an end. Adult time, unlike childhood time, is long in minutes but short in years. Hours last for years, but years go by in seconds. On the last day of class I hand back portfolios and give my students a tentative final grade. I have been dreading my confrontation with Dolores all morning but since it is the last day, I am also feeling something akin to hope, like hope with opposite particle spin. When Dolores comes in and gets the bad news, she leaves without incident or complaint, and I take my first full-body breath since the day I met her in September. It's over. It's really over. There is snow on the ground and Chicago looks Midwestern for a moment in that predictably pastoral way which is both true and beside the point. But I should have known better. By the time I return to my office, there is already a phone message waiting for me. I have been summoned to the office of the same Dean, the one who listened with so much sympathy and then refused to help me.

Apparently Dolores had already been in to complain that she was going to fail the class. I had anticipated this, so I kept a file of all our email exchanges to demonstrate all the work I had put in to try and help her achieve a passing grade. I had photocopies of all her papers to show that they were not passing, that they never had been close to passing. I brought in her portfolio, which in our department is graded by two other faculty members, and showed that they too had failed her. The Dean looked at my evidence and said Dolores was going to claim the other students were constantly distracting her and that I didn't do anything about it. When I reminded her that she had been the one to assault a student, the dean neither denied it nor corroborated it. She said it was up to me. If I gave her a C, she would go away. She added that Dolores had a record of complaints and would most likely make my life difficult. And then I was dismissed.

As I sat in that chair, I thought once more of Lovemore. He had lived in Virunga National Park for years after the tragedy with his family and managed to survive the fighting in Congo. I was remembering the discussion we had about a short essay by Jane Goodall, and the amazing story he told the class. Normally I would have doubted the veracity of such a story, but he was a person without guile, so I didn't have any good reason not to believe him. The essay describes Goodall's attempts to get close to the chimps in Gombe, and Lovemore said that he had experienced the same thing with chimps in Virunga. I kind of laughed it off at first but he explained that over a long period of time, he inched closer and closer, like Goodall did—allowing the chimps to get accustomed to having him in their territory—until they basically accepted him as one of the troop. The chimps would come and spy on him and sometimes steal fruit he left unguarded. Anything with a bright color would be gone. They were very curious, he said, and loved causing mischief. One young chimp in particular would throw anything he could get his hands on at Lovemore, and then he'd laugh if he managed to hit him. Apparently his aim was pretty good too. Eventually they became comfortable enough to build nests near Lovemore's camp where they would sometimes nap during the day.

One morning, Lovemore said he woke to the sound of the chimps screaming and making a terrific noise, and he was afraid some poachers or some other predator was attacking the chimps, but it turned out one of the mothers had just given birth. He described how the entire troop seemed to be celebrating the new baby. Chimps were jumping and pulling cartwheels, playing chase. Some of the other female chimps were attempting to caress the new baby, but the young mother was having none of it. Lovemore depended on this story; it gave his time in the forest the shape of reason.

Of course, I didn't tell him the rest of Goodall's story. I didn't mention the day she watched Passion and Pom, a mother-daughter team, eat the child of a lesser female and then embrace the half-dead mother as if to say it was just business. And I didn't mention that it wasn't, as she hoped, an aberration, how she watched from her spot in a baobab tree as they did it again and again. Dominant females protect their positions in the hierarchy just like the male chimps do, with immediate and often violent results.

I want to say I failed Dolores. I want to say Dolores forgave my failure. I want to say Lovemore saved the day. I want to say I survived in Virunga among the chimps. I want to say I quit right there and stormed off in righteous anger. I want to say I was illuminated.

## 3

# Getting Fired from the Assembly Line

### By Vickie Fang

Wei touched her shoulder as he crawled beneath the blankets, then slid his hand the length of her back, down to the softness of her thighs. "What's this?" he whispered happily. "Naked?"

Ai Mei wiggled all the way to the edge of their king sized bed. "Maybe," she whispered back.

Wei reached for her. "Now I can't find you! Where's the smart girl?"

It had been a long time since Wei called her that. More than a year, perhaps. And the words, coming now in the darkness of their bed, made Ai Mei remember too vividly the first time he had used them.

"Why do you want the smart girl?" she asked. "Do you need friction?"

Wei emitted a low rumble of deeply satisfied laughter.

"Yes!" he said. "I need friction! I need *so much* friction."

"I'll go get the flour then." Ai Mei pretended to get out of the bed. Wei lunged forward, still laughing, and caught her wrist. He pulled her back to him.

"Not that kind of friction," he whispered. "The other kind."

Ai Mei buried her face against her husband's chest. She closed her eyes. "Well any old girl could give you the other kind. Why do you want the smart girl?"

You can pretend almost anything in the bedroom. Even that you're back in the factory again, and that a man you've never seen before has found out what you've done. If you are unhappy enough you want to pretend that he still looks at you the way he did the first time and that all the years of silence and disappointment that followed that day were nothing but one long string of misunderstandings.

"I want the smart girl so my engine doesn't break down," Wei whispered. He began to stroke her hip with his left hand. "Don't let it! Don't let it break down!"

Ai Mei shifted slightly and pressed her legs together hard. "Maybe you just want to expose her in front of everyone. Maybe you just want to get her fired."

Wei *had* gotten her fired. It happened when Ai Mei was in her last, worst job of all before she left Fujian, working at a factory putting the coverings on car seats with nineteen other women. Wei had come to China with a team sent to evaluate the ancient plant for a possible purchase, and he had been intrigued to learn that the piecemeal workers in Ai Mei's section earned substantially more than everyone else because their assembly line never broke down.

Wei kissed his wife's neck near the collar bone the way she liked. "Maybe she's already exposed," Wei said. "Maybe I want to get her fired *up*."

Wei had opened up the machinery and discovered what Ai Mei already knew – that the clutch needed more friction, not less. Wet flour lodged between the axle and the gears improved the assembly line so much that the women who riveted the long sheets of naugahyde could afford to wear lipstick if they wanted and supplement the rancid cafeteria food with weekly trips to the city markets and bowls of pig belly soup. Without thinking, Wei told the factory managers that one of their workers had fixed the problems with the clutch.

Ai Mei, who lay with her head still pressed against her husband's chest as if for protection, remembered the fear that had seized her the day the big bosses stormed into the women's sleeping room shouting, "Who did this? Who put paste in the clutch? Where is the woman who tried to break the assembly line?" Ai Mei, still in her pajamas, pressed her hands against the ancient mattress to keep them from trembling. She heard a frightened whimper from the woman whose bed was above her own, and she wondered if the Bosses could do more than fire her. Could they put her in jail too?

"Where you glad I was the one?" she asked Wei. "That day? You know, when it happened?"

"Glad," Wei whispered back. He was working his way up her neck. She could feel his breath in her ear, the warm touch of his lips.

Ai Mei had already begun walking forward, about to denounce herself before everyone else was blamed too, when the Chinese American man came running in behind them. He had a big smile plastered across his frightened face. "Yes!" he said in his extremely limited Fukinese dialect. "Where is she? Where is the smart girl?" Then he turned to one of the bosses and said in quiet, rapid Mandarin, "It's very important to reward initiative. I'm sure that's what you want to do, *reward* the woman who figured this all out."

He had stood in the middle of the squalid women's dormitory like an apparition with his American suit and tie and his foolish hope that he could convince these men not to be angry at a woman who jeopardized the entire line by putting paste in the clutch. "Where is the smart girl?" he cried again, as if the other men had come to congratulate Ai Mei for her cleverness rather than to punish her, severely, for being a female assembly line worker who interfered with the machines without permission. The absurdity of the entire situation – of the foreigner who had actually believed that he could help, of the managers too arrogant and stupid to recognize even the most obvious benefit of having employees who could think, of herself most of all for having managed her life so poorly that she ended up working in a place as miserable as this one – struck her with a sudden and almost blinding force. *Why*, she asked herself, *do I care about any of them?* And then, as she had said to herself before in other, far less horrible positions, *Fuck this job anyway.*

Ai Mei passed the last of the long row of metal bunk beds. She stopped, looked the American Chinese directly in the face, and gestured with one steady, dismissive hand at the enraged Bosses.

"Smarter than these men?" she asked. "Is that what you mean by 'smart girl'? Well, then, thank you so much for the big, big compliment."

For five seconds, longer, perhaps, the entire room fell into a shocked silence. The biggest Boss actually seemed frightened. He took a step backwards in the narrow aisle between bunks, his face brushing up against a little clothesline of drying white underpants. The other women, still sitting on their mattresses, looked down. Some put their hands over their faces. Then Wei, whose career would never again include any kind of foreign negotiations, burst into a howl of delighted laughter.

Now when he touched her, Ai Mei liked to pretend that she could still hear the laughter from that moment in the dorm and still see his admiring look. Some days made her want to pretend very hard.

*Getting Fired from the Assembly Line is an excerpt from Vickie Fang's soon to be completed novel, The Believers, in which two antagonists from the Chinese Cultural Revolution settle scores in contemporary America. The book is kind of an Amy Tan meets Breaking Bad. Getting Fired from the Assembly Line gives readers a preview of the appallingly big mouth of one of the characters.*

# Life in the Dungeon

## By Johnny Townsend

I saw the short, hunchbacked woman shuffling toward the booth and waved her over. She was elderly and would probably want to buy November's senior bus pass for $27. As she drew closer to the window, I could see that her left eye looked off severely to the side. I wondered if she could even see with it.

"How can I help you?" I asked cheerfully.

"There's shit in the elevator. A huge pile of it. I stepped right in it, and I couldn't get it off my shoe."

I looked at the floor behind her and could see that she was telling the truth. She was tracking something repulsive along as she walked. "I'll report it to the Facilities guys immediately."

"You know why they did it, don't you?" said the woman. "They're mad that you got rid of the Ride Free Zone."

I was a Bus Pass Sales Rep for Seattle Transit. Three weeks earlier, the city had eliminated its policy of allowing anyone to ride for free within the downtown area, a program which had lasted forty years. The city could no longer afford it. Some pointed out that making it harder to get around downtown would discourage both tourists and locals from shopping, and the city would lose even more revenue than it would gain by charging $2.25 per ride. That was yet to be determined, but already known was that many, many people were unhappy.

And now someone had protested in the Transit elevator at the Westlake station.

Transit only had two offices, our main one near Pioneer Square, and the one where I worked, in the tunnel at Westlake on the other end of the downtown area. Seattle had long ago created a transit tunnel underground going the length of downtown, from Westlake on the north, not far from the Space Needle, to the International District on the south in Chinatown. A dozen different bus lines, plus the light rail, avoided street traffic by operating below the surface. Sometimes, I felt like a Morlock servicing the Eloi.

"I think you got the winner for the day," said Tim, one of my coworkers. There were three of us working the tiny booth about the size of a handicapped bathroom stall. I felt I was spending my days in an airplane cockpit. The only festive feature was a garland of orange skeletons draped along the top of the Plexiglass windows. Tim weighed about 300 pounds and took insulin every day, usually in pill form but sometimes by injection. Every afternoon during break, he would bring back Halloween candy and hand it to the rest of us, saying he at least wanted vicarious pleasure. The only proxy work I could do, I thought, since I no longer held a temple recommend.

"You didn't see my customer?" asked Sharon, a hefty 240 pounds herself. She was divorced and always talking badly about her ex. "The woman had $200 on her card and was complaining about being overcharged twenty-five cents on a bus. I had to do a goddamn cash adjustment for twenty-five cents."

Cash adjustments were tedious, I had to admit, often taking fifteen minutes. I did five or six of them a day, usually for teenaged Chinese girls who'd accidentally bought an adult card and put a youth pass on it, where it wouldn't work. The card was never registered, which meant I had to spend a few minutes registering it, not easy because I had to get the address of the girl, always difficult because of her limited English. Then I'd have to refund the card, issue a new card and register that one, and then transfer the funds over. Not the end of the world, but tiresome, especially since a whole gang of girls would usually come just a few minutes before closing.

"Yes, your customer was a pain in the butt," I said to Sharon. Sharon sometimes worked as a senior, our word for supervisor, and I didn't want to get on her bad side. She routinely read her mail, clipped coupons, read the newspaper, played on the internet, filled out forms so her sons could attend various activities, ate popcorn, and did all sorts of other inappropriate things at her window. When customers would come to her station, she'd take a minute before looking up from whatever she was doing, and then she'd look back down and continue her personal activities, ignoring the customer. The customer would glance around in confusion, and I'd wave them over to my window. Even when Sharon did address the customer, it was usually with an antagonistic tone to her voice. I didn't personally see the advantage in being a creep, even if it was all displaced anger at one's ex.

Of course, I didn't have an ex. I was still with my first love.

"I don't know why people have to be such jerks," she said. "Must be a full moon."

"Only a week or so until Halloween," said Tim. "The nuts'll be crawling out of the woodwork before long." He was turned toward us, his back to his window, and he didn't see the young Hispanic woman walking up to him. "You and your partner celebrate Halloween, Graydon?"

I nodded and then pointed to his window. Tim turned and jumped in surprise when he saw the woman standing there. "Thanks," he said to me after he'd helped her. "She was hot."

Sharon ignored us and kept painting her nails.

"Oh, my mother will probably haunt me for saying that." Tim was 57 and had lived with his mother till she died nine months ago. He'd never married but was always talking about the "young chicks" who came to his window, or the strip clubs he frequented on weekends. "Every time I lust after a girl, Mom sends a pregnant woman my way to keep me in line." He looked into the tunnel and pointed out a pregnant woman in a burqa coming up off an escalator. "See?"

"You know, there's therapy for that," I said.

"Oh, I don't mean she's really haunting me," said Tim. "I'm not hearing voices or anything. What do Mormons believe about ghosts?"

"We believe they pretty much leave us alone," I said.

"Do you still believe in God, even after being excommunicated?"

I'd been ex'ed two years before, a week after my 25th birthday. Tim had never gotten over it. He wasn't religious but thought excommunication was barbaric. "You've been in a relationship for a year," he'd told me at the time.

"That's already longer than anything I've had. How can they say you're a monster?" He was still marveling that I'd been with Alex for three years now.

My parents were still marveling that I'd chosen a Jewish partner. Growing up, I had only known Anglo-Saxons from the congregation I'd been a part of for so many years. Even now, my parents knew only one non-Anglo personally, Alex.

An elderly man came up to my window. "What can I do for you?"

"I'd like a senior transit card."

"How old are you?"

He handed me an Indonesian ID card. "I'm 64."

"Oh, then you'll need to come back when you turn 65."

Right then, two more people came to my window one after another, the first shifting over from Sharon's window where she wasn't being helped. I loaded $30 onto one card for a Danish exchange student and put a $90 regular adult November pass on another for a Japanese woman. I liked these transactions. People usually paid with cash or credit, so it was a quick, easy task. A couple of times a day, customers paid with vouchers from some company or charity paying their fare, and those took a little longer to process, but even those were relatively simple transactions. Actually, most of what we did every day was pretty easy. The only thing I didn't like was that I had to stand on my feet all day. Tim and Sharon sat in chairs, but I found that if I sat, I couldn't reach the window or the receipt printer or the calculator. I had to move around and reach for too many things during every transaction. Sometimes, it was easier to do the harder thing.

"So you still believe?" asked Tim. He wasn't going to let it drop.

I knew that Sharon's oldest son was studying theology at Gonzaga in Spokane and thinking of becoming a Catholic priest. Alex attended Torah study on Saturdays but rarely attended services. "Sure, I believe," I said.

Even if the last thing I heard my stake president say was, "You're on your own now. Don't ask the Church for any help when you get in trouble." I nodded at Hector, the janitor, as he walked by the booth. He nodded back.

"Oh, that's good," Tim replied.

"Why?"

"I'd hate to see religion hurt you."

I laughed. "It's already hurt me."

"Will you guys shut up?" said Sharon. "I'm trying to read." She could barely hold on to her magazine with her fingers spread wide so her nails could dry.

I waved a man standing in front of her window over to mine. "Can I help you?" I asked.

The man thrust a transit card at me. "Money," he said in a thick Middle Eastern accent.

I put the card on the reader and saw that he had $2.25 left on his card. I told him the amount.

"Money," he said again.

"Did you want to put money on the card?" I asked.

"Huh?" He looked confused. "Money," he repeated.

"What about money?" I asked.

"Money," he said again with more conviction.

I held out my hand. He still looked confused but handed me a twenty dollar bill.

"You want me to put twenty on the card?" I asked.

He pointed to the bill.

I loaded the money onto the card and gave him his receipt with his card. He nodded brusquely and headed off.

"Oh, I got another hot girl," said Tim. An auburn-haired woman was approaching his station.

"You know, they can hear you over your microphone," said Sharon. She put down her magazine and waved impatiently for a woman with a stroller to come to her window. "Can I help you?" she said in a strained voice.

We'd already taken our morning breaks, and soon Tim took the first lunch, at 11:15. He didn't return for an hour, and I left at 12:20. It could be dreary working underground all day. I felt safe from nuclear attack, but that was about the only positive aspect of working in the tunnel. I worried that an earthquake would trap me in the booth, and I'd spend my last two weeks dying in the rubble, unable to escape Tim and Sharon. On some days, I felt buried alive in a tight coffin.

Alex usually made my lunch, a turkey sandwich or peanut butter and jelly. Today I had turkey with a slice of dill pickle, a surprise treat. I could have eaten in the tiny break room behind the counter, an area about the size of a small walk-in closet, but I needed to get away. On sunny days, I sat on a bench outside in front of the Westlake Shopping Center, but as it was raining today, I just went to the third floor food court and grabbed an empty table.

I still thought of religion more than I wanted to. Could I truly be a good person without it? Or was I really the horror the Church said I was? Dracula never saw himself as evil. The Mummy felt completely justified in the murders he was committing. It was only an objective person looking on from the outside who could see the truth. On my mission to Minnesota, my companions and I had had a motto: You have to apostatize to baptize. Sometimes, you simply had to break the rules to do the right thing. I'd tried to leave Mormonism behind me, but I still sent a yearly protest letter to Salt Lake, and of course I donated to the Human Rights Campaign, Lambda Legal, the ACLU, and the Southern Poverty Law Center. Still, I wasn't very much of an activist. I'd been contacted by the organization "Mormons for Marriage Equality" in regard to the Washington State campaign to legalize gay marriage here, and I'd written some emails to my elected officials as well as a couple of letters to the editor to complain about the Church pushing its members to vote against equality. I was grateful to see the handful of straight, supposedly faithful Mormons who were standing up for us, but frankly, I didn't much care if they liked me or not. Part of me cheered the gay Mormons who picketed in front of temples and held kiss-ins on Temple Square. Another part of me didn't give a shit. The Church often gloated, "You can't leave us alone," as if that somehow proved their divine status, but in reality, it was the Church who couldn't leave *us* alone.

So Romney scared me. I'd already turned in my mail-in vote for Obama, but the race was still neck and neck in battleground states across the country. The prospect of a Mormon president who wanted to ban gay marriage and abortion and who was part of a party that wanted to dismantle Social Security and Medicare was terrifying. My family emailed me about how Romney was going to save the Constitution which was "hanging by a thread." I worried that the relative acceptance gays had in society now could be ripped away overnight. Alex had told me just last evening, "I wonder if this was how the Jews felt right before the election where Hitler took control." Romney was no Hitler, but persecution was persecution. Even if he didn't win, another awful Republican with Draconian ideas was sure to follow him.

I looked around at the people in the food court. Several Asian youths were sitting at the table next to me, eating noodles with chopsticks. A heavy white woman with mussed up dirty blond hair was eating a pulled pork sandwich a few tables away. A businessman in a suit was eating a McChicken sandwich. A thin brunette was eating a salad and two black teenage girls were slurping Smoothies. An Ethiopian woman in a purple head scarf was eating rice and broccoli.

America was a great place, I thought, where all these people could come together in peace.

So why did I always feel such an impending sense of doom?

I looked out the window at the rain misting down and luxuriated in being able to sit for a full forty-five minutes, even on a hard chair.

Once I was back in the booth, Sharon took off without a word. My first customer was an elderly Russian woman who wanted to put $20 on her card. "Spaseba," I said when she'd finished.

She laughed and said, "Pajalsta." I could never remember which term meant thanks and which meant you're welcome. But the elderly Russian women who came to the booth always got a kick out of even my one Russian word.

A Vietnamese woman stopped by to purchase a book of ten $1.25 youth fare tickets. I was sure she was buying them for herself and trying to pass off to bus drivers that she was still a teenager.

"You and your partner doing anything for Halloween?" asked Tim during a brief lull. "Going to any haunted houses?"

"I doubt it. You?"

"My mother loved Halloween. When I was a month old, she put me in a basket, put a note that said, 'Please take care of me' on top, and left me on the neighbor's porch. She rang his doorbell and then hid in the bushes and watched him almost faint when he found me. Then she jumped out and said, 'Scared you on Halloween!'"

"Your mother sounds very special."

"Oh, she was, she was. She's still with me. Look! There's another pregnant woman." He pointed.

A Hispanic man came to my window then and plopped down his card. "Want month," he said.

"You want the November pass?" I asked.

"Month." He nodded.

He had a regular adult card, which meant he was eligible for the $81 pass, the $90 pass, the $99 pass, the $108 pass, and on up to $126. "Which one?"

"Month." He said it firmly and nodded authoritatively.

I looked up Details to see if he'd had a pass in the preceding months. Then I could just get him whatever he'd bought before. I saw the screen and took a breath. He'd had both an $81 pass and a $90 pass. "You want the $81 pass?"

"Yes. Pass."

"Did you want the $90 pass?"

"Pass. Yes."

I held out my hand, hopeful the answer would come in whatever the man pushed through the slot in the window. But no, he handed me a $100 bill. I marked it with my counterfeit pen to verify it. "$90?" I asked.

He nodded. I put the pass on the card and handed him the card, his receipt, and $10. He looked confused and walked off.

"You're really good with the customers," said Tim. "I get so impatient."

"Can I help you?" I waved at a 40-year-old white woman with stringy hair who looked as if she couldn't decide whether or not to approach. She did.

The woman thrust her application for a Disability card through my window. "The FBI wants this," she said. "And Jesus wants it."

"I'm afraid we don't process these here," I said. "The Disabled cards are printed at our main branch in Pioneer Square." I slid the paper back to her. She pushed it right back at me again.

"You keep it. I'll lose it. The FBI wants it. Satan wants it, too." She shuffled away slowly like a zombie.

I took the form and went back to the senior's office. Mike was watching a football game on the internet. "Can we interoffice this to the main branch so the customer will have it when she shows up to get a card? She doesn't want to keep it. She's afraid she'll lose it."

Mike took the form, looked at it for a few seconds, and then put it on his desk where dozens of other miscellaneous papers lay. "They have no place to keep these. She'll need to bring another." He turned back to his game.

I returned to my window and put thirty dollars on a youth card for a petite blonde teenager.

"She was hot," said Tim after the girl left.

"She was fifteen."

Soon Sharon was back at her window, sipping coffee. The only time she really helped was when she had to sell taxi scrip, since she was the only cashier allowed to sell it. Taxi scrip was a type of coupon that allowed the customer to buy a certain amount of taxi fare for half price, say $30 for $15 or $50 for $25. People had to have a special yellow card to be eligible.

At the beginning and end of each month, our line out front might get up to fifty people in length, but at this time of the cycle it was never more than four or five long, and sometimes there was no line at all. It was the longest it had been all day right now, with four people waiting for their turn. A thirty-year-old bypassed the other four people and came around from the side directly to my window. "Uh, there's a line," I said, smiling and pointing.

"But the sign said to step to the side if you wanted to avoid the line."

There were two signs on either side of the line, which directed customers to the Regional Transit vending machines along the walls to buy cards, load cards, or buy light rail tickets. All of that could be done without us, yet a great many people came to us anyway. "If you read the sign more carefully," I said, still smiling, "you'll see that it isn't an invitation to cut in line." I pointed for her to go to the back of the group.

She turned around, bewildered, and wandered away.

"You were too nice," Sharon muttered. "That little bitch knew exactly what she was doing."

Some days, I wondered if being cast into Outer Darkness when I died would mean having to live like this for eternity. If the Church were right about gays, it would be worth being celibate for sixty years to avoid such a fate. The devil wasn't scary only at the end of October.

Stop it, Graydon, I told myself. You're over this. You're over it.

"Boy, that was some good looking gal," said Tim, turned around in his chair so that he was facing Sharon and me rather than his window. I didn't even know which woman he was referring to. Sharon ignored him and kept looking at pictures on her phone. It was Tim's turn to take his afternoon break and he put up a sign in front of his window. "Maybe I'll follow her for a while."

"Think of your mother," I said, to ward off the stalking. Tim looked at the floor glumly and went to sit in the back room instead. I saw a young woman walk purposefully toward the booth and thought about letting Sharon take her. It was Satan's plan, though, to try to force people to be good rather than let them choose. I waved her over.

"My transit card broke," said the woman with difficulty. She had some kind of speech impediment. She thrust the card at me. It was a green and white Disability card that allowed the rider to pay seventy-five cents per fare.

"I'm afraid we don't print those at this location," I said. "You'll need to go to the main branch near Pioneer Square."

"They told me I could come here," she said with a whine, instantly petulant. Her mouth twitched.

"I'm sorry about the misinformation, but we simply don't have a printer that can print those here."

"Well, what am I going to do?" She was raising her voice.

"You're going to need to go down to the main branch."

"But I have a seizure disorder. You have to accommodate me."

"Ma'am, our printer won't print those cards. There's nothing we can do at this location."

"I don't think you understand. I'm disabled."

"Yes, and the branch that handles Disability applications and prints Disability cards is our main branch near Pioneer Square."

"I can't go all the way down there!" She was yelling now, drawing looks from the other people in line behind her and from passersby walking toward the stairs leading down to the bus and train platform. "I have my paperwork *here*!" She threw it at me. The papers hit the window and then fell on the floor.

"Ma'am, you're welcome to yell and argue as long as you wish, but that's not going to change anything."

I instantly realized that this was exactly the same message the Church was sending to me when it ignored our protests. Some things were simply pointless. I glanced over briefly at Sharon. Was being second-class going to be my fate the rest of my life, both in and out of the Church? What if the election in a couple of weeks made Washington the 32nd state in a row to deny marriage equality? Even my own family lovingly demonized me.

The woman slapped the counter, and I turned back to her, irritated for allowing myself to be distracted by my own thoughts. "You can get a friend or family member to help you get there if you're having difficulty on your own. We also have the Access van if you need it."

"Give me the number of the main office!"

I wrote down our Customer Service number.

"Not that one! The direct line!"

"We don't give out the direct line. You can call this number, and they'll transfer you."

"I WANT THE DIRECT NUMBER!"

"This is what I can give you." I slipped the note paper through the little opening in my window, and she pushed it back.

"I need the manager's direct number!" she repeated. "I can't go all the way to the other branch!"

"Ma'am," I said quietly into my microphone. "Blind people go down there. People without legs go down there. You're a big girl. You can handle it."

"Stop talking into that damn microphone! You're going to make me seize!"

I turned off the microphone and said through the thick glass, "You're going to need to step away from the window."

"What?" She leaned forward.

"You're going to need to—"

"Huh?"

I turned the microphone back on. "You're going to need to step away and let me wait on the other customers."

"Well, you haven't helped *me* yet!"

"I've told you where you need to go to accomplish what you want, and I've given you our customer service number. You're going to need to step away."

"You can tell her where to go all right," Sharon muttered next to me.

The woman continued to yell, and I turned my microphone back off so I wouldn't have to hear her. Then I walked to the senior's office and said to Mike, "I need help out here. I have an irate customer who won't leave." I explained the situation, and he walked through the two locked doors separating our booth from the tunnel. I waited until I saw him lead the woman off, and then I returned to my window.

"I almost felt sorry for you," said Sharon, leaning over.

Almost, I thought. My own instincts were to feel bad for anyone disabled and go out of my way to make their lives easier, but some disabled people used their disability like a weapon and tried to bully everyone in their path. I'd come close to saying, "I understand that you're unhappy and that this leads you to want to make everyone around you unhappy, but no matter how much you yell, I'm not going to be able to help you." I'd been afraid she'd report me, though, so I'd tried to maintain my composure.

Then a new thought struck me. Were gays using *our* "disability" like a weapon, too?

I remembered one obnoxious customer at my window justifying her behavior to me a couple of weeks ago, "Well-behaved women rarely make history." I'd wanted to say then, "No one's going to remember you, either. You're just a bitter old asshole who makes everyone around you miserable, and in a few years you're going to die and be forgotten. Being poorly behaved doesn't make you important. Or right." But I knew she'd have reported me, too, so I just kept a blank face and let her gloat.

Was I like that when I wrote to the Church?

I looked at the ring on my hand, which I wore despite the lack of a marriage certificate. Even with this crummy job that took up most of my waking life, I still had Alex to go home to.

I looked out and saw Mike turning away from the woman, and watched her defeated expression as her right hand twitched. There was no way I could offer to take her to the other branch on Saturday, my day off, because both branches were closed the same days. I'd already had my lunch break today, so I couldn't use that to help her down to Pioneer Square now. Sharon was next to me, playing with an ink pen which had a skull on top that lit up whenever she pressed down. She kept lighting it while an Indian man at her window talked.

The disabled woman was still standing motionless in the tunnel.

Why did I even feel obligated to help this unpleasant customer staring dejectedly at the floor in the first place? Because I knew it must be harder to *be* her than simply to deal with her? Because I wanted some Mormon somewhere to be nice to me? Even a blind man had the power to pour soup for Frankenstein's monster.

I locked my computer and passed Mike on his way back through the metal doors. "Where are you going?" he asked. "Isn't Tim on break?"

"I'm going to escort that woman to the main branch. I'll be back in thirty minutes, forty minutes tops. You can dock my hours."

"Are you kidding me?"

"Hey, I'm all alone up here," Sharon shouted into the hallway where we were standing.

"Be back in a jiffy, Mike. Thanks." I smiled and nodded, not waiting for his reply, and headed out the door.

# 5

# Call Center

### By Noel Osualdini

*You'd think that spending all day on the phone in an air-conditioned office would be the ultimate cushy job. But the call center operator is stuck between management, who are under pressure to control costs, and customers who want the best possible service. Call center staff are often harassed, belittled and occasionally brought to tears by abusive and demanding clients. Sometimes, it almost seems as if the callers are out for blood.*

By mid-morning, there would be a definite hum in the center, a buzz that customer service consultant Alan Perry had learned to ignore. At ten o'clock, the second shift would come on board; by mid-morning, the sound of a hundred people chattering at their desks would become white noise. Right now, he could still make out the individual voices of some of his colleagues: Rob, struggling to make himself understood by a caller who was either deaf, foreign or just stupid; Colin, making an appointment for a serviceman to meet the customer at his premises; Julie with a late payer whose electricity had been disconnected.

"But you haven't paid anything in six months," Julie was saying, while Rob was explaining the impact that a big, new plasma TV might make on an electricity bill, and Colin was concluding: "He'll meet you at the front of the house at one thirty tomorrow afternoon. If you're not there to meet him, madam, I'm afraid he'll just go to his next appointment."

At tea break, Alan might toss a joke at Rob or Colin; after work he might have a beer with colleagues at the bar across the back lane; and tonight he might fuck Julie. Last night had been too desperate, too hurried, both of them tearing at each others' clothes before the apartment door had even closed properly.

But right now, he was saying to a Mr Russell of Carnegie: "Yes, I understand that the electricity meter was due to be read a few days ago. The readings haven't come in yet, but..." He was flipping through the information on the screen before him – "...I'll just send an email to our billing department, and they'll get a bill out to you in about a week or two...No, it'll have to go through the post...no, I won't be calling you when the reading comes in...Yes, thank you for calling, Mr Russell."

He pushed a button on his phone to terminate the call. He was supposed to wait for the customer to hang up, but old people were notoriously slow. There was a two second interval of silence, then a beep indicating the next call was about to come down the line.

A young woman on the other end launched without preamble into a complaint about a reminder she'd received, screeching and swearing, and he pulled the padded earpiece away.

\* \* \*

"These bloody customers will be the death of me, I swear," Alan said. "Old people always whine they can't pay their bills, but they always ring up to complain if it's not in their mailbox the day after the reading."

"Nothing better to do with their time," Rob said.

"And if you don't pay your bill, well yeah, we'll cut off your power."

"I spoke with Garry Matthews today," said Julie.

"What, the television actor?" asked Rob, taking the beer glass from his mouth.

"Well, famous people use electricity too."

"What'd he want?" asked Alan.

"Something about being charged for a mercury lamp in his garden that hasn't worked in years."

"Get him to write in and then you can have his autograph," said Colin.

"I'd never keep original correspondence from a customer," said Julie, smiling, "even if it *was* Garry Matthews. You know that." But the grin told them that she would.

"I spoke to a man called Rich Nixon once," said Rob. "Now *that* would be a good autograph to have."

"Especially since he's been dead for years."

"Richard Nixon isn't dead. He's alive and kicking," said Colin.

"And living in the same street as Elvis," Rob added.

For a couple of minutes they debated whether the former president was, in fact, still alive.

"I spoke to a John Ford once," said Alan. "And one day I even had a call from Robert Burns."

"Who?" asked Rob.

"A Scottish poet," Julie said.

"I spoke to a Johnny Walker last week," laughed Rob. "Hey, did you hear they're advertising a 2IC position for our team? Second in charge. Are you going to go for it, Al?"

"Reckon I might have a chance," replied Alan.

"Well, you've been here longer than most of us."

Somebody called across the bar, and they all looked up – but it was nobody they knew.

"And with that," said Rob, draining his glass, "I'll go grab the next round."

* * *

"Hello, you're speaking to – "

"This is Mr Russell in Carnegie" said an angry voice on the phone. Abrupt. Demanding. "I spoke to you last week."

"I speak to a lot of people," Alan replied cheerily, readjusting the volume on his headset. He typed in some details and waited for the account information to appear. The guy was obviously old: grouchy, forthright, the type that would call back later to complain about him if he wasn't satisfied. A little voice emerging from the static on the line told him that Mrs Russell was probably hovering behind her husband and that he'd have to be prepared to take a berating from her, too.

"It was definitely you," said Mr Russell. "*Alan.*"

That threw him for a moment; he hadn't given his name yet. He asked for the account number.

"You have a good memory for voices, sir," he commented, scrolling through the information.

"Where's my bill?" asked the old man, impatiently. "You told me a week ago that I'd have it and it's still not here."

"I'm just looking now."

"Have you got me on the computer, Alan?" asked Mr Russell.

"I'm just checking."

"Not there? Then what's the good of it?" Sarcastically: "Do you need to change screens, Alan? Send an email? Put me on hold for five minutes while you check with somebody? You promised me it would be here this week."

Frantically, Alan was searching through the notes on the account, and found that Mr Russell had spoken to two other customer service officers in the past few days.

*How the hell does he remember me?* he wondered. As he read quickly through the call logs in the account, he found his own abbreviated note to Billing: MTR RD NOT AVAIL. PLS CHK AND SEND BILL

"I'll get on to it straight away," Alan promised.

"Well see that you do, young man."

But as soon as Mr Russell banged the phone down, another call dropped onto the line, and Alan had to scribble a note to himself to follow the matter up later.

* * *

Julie tried to drag him away from the kitchen table where he'd been composing his application for the 2IC position.

"No, I've got to finish this."

"But I've got something for you," she said seductively.

"How well do I deal with conflict?" he asked, reading from the job criteria.

"Don't ask *me*, I'm not the one going for the job," she replied. "Just say anything."

"I know I can deal with people – it's just a matter of coming up with the sort of thing they're expecting to hear."

"Try dealing with this," she said, rubbing a breast against him. He shook her off, and she took a step back. "You *know* you can do the job, and there shouldn't be any other serious contenders – unless they go outside."

"No, they only take team leaders from outside," Alan reminded her. "2ICs are supposed to know the whole system backwards. Team leaders are just interested in keeping everyone in line." He rubbed his eyes with the back of a hand and held the page up to reread it, yawning.

"Come on," said Julie. "Bedtime for you, tiger."

She growled suggestively, and he forgot about writing any more of his application for the moment.

* * *

Mr Russell called again. The bill was wrong.

"Do you just guess how much electricity we've used?"

Checking the comments on the computer, Alan said: "There's a reading in your records, Mr Russell, but it's an estimate."

"*Estimate?*" It was almost an exasperated shout. "Why is it an estimate?"

Alan opened another program to check the meaning of a particular code shown against the reading.

"*Gate locked*," he read.

"What?"

"You've got a locked gate. We can't send you an accurate bill if we can't get in to read the meter."

"Then why send me a bill at all?"

Alan had had this conversation countless times before. "We're obliged by law to issue a bill every three months," he explained. "But if the meter reader can't get in because of a gate or a savage dog, we have to estimate how much power you've used."

"My dog died a year ago!"

"I can book an appointment for you," Alan said. He glanced at his screen: the display indicated there were fifty other callers trying to get through to an operator. He sighed unintentionally.

"Is that a hint of hostility I'm hearing from you, young man? Don't you get all huffy and puffy over the phone at me. What's your surname? I might just have to put in a complaint about you."

Alan apologized while he consulted a list of available appointment times.

"Is ten a.m. on Wednesday okay? Please leave the gate open. I'll leave instructions for the reader to knock on the door when he gets there."

He clicked a button to enter a request, and typed in the instructions for the meter reader: APPT 10 AM WED: KNOCK ON DOOR FOR ACCESS, READ METER

"I asked for your surname, young man," said Mr Russell.

"It's company policy that we don't give out our surnames, I'm afraid."

"Afraid? What are you afraid of? Afraid you might be held accountable? Afraid an old man might look you up in the phone book and come around and give you what-for for not doing your job?"

"I *am* doing my job, sir."

After Mr Russell banged the phone down, a beep in Alan's earpiece indicated the next call was about to drop in to his line.

* * *

"Do you ever regret not finishing your degree?" asked Julie, lying beside him in bed. Lately, their conversations had revolved around work and career and what could have been. Although he was only twenty six, Alan wondered sometimes whether this was what it was like to be married and middle aged and bored with life.

"It was just an Arts degree."

"But you could have added that education diploma. You'd be a teacher by now."

"I never would have met you." He kissed her on the nose.

"You never know."

"I'd probably be bored out of my brain."

"*Good morning, Mr Pare-ree,*" she chanted, as school children would.

"Why are you asking?"

"*Can I leave the room, Mr Pare-ree?*"

"No, seriously..." He was a little annoyed at her schoolgirl imitation. "I'm never going into teaching. Why did you ask about my degree?"
She shook her head. "The look on your face last week when nobody knew who Robert Burns was..."

He recalled the conversation. "I'm surprised they knew who John Ford was."

"Yeah, he invented the Ford motor car, didn't he?"

Alan didn't doubt she knew the difference between the car manufacturer and the man who'd directed countless cowboy movies, or why Robert Frost was a famous name. But he was silent for a minute.

"I don't think any of them are ever going to go far...Rob and Colin and the rest," Julie mused. "They just don't seem to have the ambition to do anything else."

"*Ah, the best-laid schemes o' mice an' men gang aft agley,*" Alan replied, quoting Frost. He was thoughtful. "When one of my teachers asked us to write about what we wanted to do when we grew up, I said I wanted to be a journalist."

"I never knew you could write — journalism write, I mean."

"I didn't want to be a journalist, really. I didn't have a clue what I wanted to do. I just sort of fell into the idea of being a teacher. It all seemed so unreal...It seemed like there were years before we had to make a decision and eventually, teaching became a last resort. But I got bored with that idea, too."

"So push for the 2IC job," she urged. "That's just one step below team leader. Eventually, they've got to start recruiting team leaders from staff."

"I can't imagine anyone saying his ambition was to be second in charge of a team in a call center."

"Or *her*."

"Or her," he agreed.

And now Julie, too, was thinking about what might have been.

"By now I could have been...supervisor for the women's underwear department," she said, recalling her last career. She shrugged. "Call center work will have to do until something better comes along, I guess." She giggled, and asked: "*Can I suck on a lollipop, Mr Pare-ree?*" She slid down under the covers.

* * *

"You had a seventeen minute conversation on Tuesday!" said Margaret, the team leader.

Alan thought about it, and recalled, "Mr Russell. He complained about an estimated reading."

"But a seventeen minute conversation, Alan! That's totally irresponsible when we've got other callers in the queue!"

"He wanted to complain about everything."

"Well I'm sorry," said Margaret, "but you're letting the team down. You'll have to pick up your feet if you want to get anywhere in this organization."

She stormed off, leaving Alan to take the next call.

During his lunch break, he went out to the balcony, and looked down at the milling people in the street below. There was a narrow ledge beyond the railing that he was standing at, and then a drop of six stories to the road. He imagined himself walking along that ledge, and then he imagined what it would be like to step off the edge: the sensation of falling, air gushing past, arms flailing to grasp at emptiness, the ground rushing up and then a thud.

And then nothing.

He suddenly felt dizzy, and leaned back from the rail.

"Whoa, buddy," said someone, grabbing his arm. "Thought you were gonna collapse."

Alan shook his head. Rob's face swam into focus.

"No, I'm okay."

"You've spilled your coffee."

Alan looked down at the polystyrene cup in his hand, and noticed the liquid still steaming on his skin.

"Yow, that's hot!" He straightened the cup.

* * *

"Alan, I have a Mr Russell on the phone for you," a young woman's voice said through his headset. She gave an account number, and brought the customer onto the line. "Thank you for holding, Mr Russell," she said, "I've got Alan for you now." A click indicated she'd hung up.

"Alan," said a strained voice, almost shouting, "I'm still waiting on my replacement bill. I'm getting a little impatient."

"It should have gone out as soon as the read came back in," Alan said, checking his own notes and the results of the meter read. In the meter reader's comments, he found: CUST NO-SHOW. WAITED 15 MINUTES. GATE LOCKED.

"You weren't there," said Alan.

"I'm an old man. I'm here all the time."

"But the notes in the computer say the meter reader waited for you."

"Did he knock at the door, or just stand at the gate?"

"I left instructions to knock at the door, but the gate was locked and he couldn't get to the front door. It was at ten o'clock Wednesday."

"Wednesday? I had a doctor's appointment Wednesday morning at nine thirty."

"But you were going to be at home to let the meter reader in."

"Let me tell you," said Mr Russell, "when you get to my age, you make damned sure you keep all of your appointments with your doctors."

"If your wife had been at home…"

"She always comes with me. Don't you tell me how to live my life. Except for this one appointment, we were waiting at home all day."

Silently, Alan shook his head.

"Would you like another appointment? The next available is…Tuesday, 11:30 a.m." He typed: APPT 11:30 AM TUE KNOCK ON DOOR FOR ACCESS READ METER

"You'd better make sure he turns up this time!" said Mr Russell, and hung up before Alan could remind him to be at home.

"Do you ever get the feeling they're out to get you?" he asked, in a break between calls.

"That's called paranoia," Julie said across the low barrier that separated their desks.

"No, it's not paranoia," said Colin. "Remember Stan Johnson? Went off to join his father's delivery business? I got a call one day from a guy who was gonna come down and knock his block off 'cos he wouldn't talk to him about his neighbour's account. But Stan was in the right. The law says – " He tapped his headset to indicate that a call was about to drop through to him, and said into his microphone: "Good morning, you're speaking to Colin. How can I help you?" He turned back to his own desk.

"I got someone who was gonna do that to me once," Rob said. "Told me he knew where I worked. The idiot was somewhere in the country, though, so I said 'Sure, I'll give you my address. Reckon you could afford the plane fare to come meet me?'"

"You never said that," said Julie, disbelieving. "If management had heard, you'd be in big trouble."

"Well, I *almost* said it. I knew a guy who worked for Social Security once," he continued. "Told everyone in his neighborhood that if they ever had any problems, they could come to see him and he'd sort it out. So one day someone must've had a problem, but instead of coming around to see him, they blew up his car."

"Lucky it was just his car."

They all agreed.

"Alan," called Margaret, his team leader, as she walked over to his desk. "About that 2IC position…"

* * *

"Are you disappointed you missed out?" Julie asked, rolling onto her belly to rest her chin on his shoulder.

The successful candidate for the job had been announced, and it wasn't Alan. Beginning next week, he'd be answering to somebody who'd been in the company three years less than he had. That night, for the first time, he'd been totally unsuccessful in bed.

"Don't worry about it," said Julie, rubbing his back. "It's not important."

He was miserable.

* * *

"I have a Terry Russell on the phone for you," said the voice on the line. "His account number is …"

Alan typed the account number into the computer "Terry Russ––" and recognized his own name in the list of contact notes. "Not this guy again. What does he want?"

"He wouldn't say. But he sounds really angry. He wants to speak to you."

"No," said Alan. "I don't want to talk to him. He complains about not getting his bill, then when he gets it he comlains it's estimated, and when I make an appointment for a reading, he isn't home, so he complains about that and I have to make another appointment…*No*," he said, with finality.

His colleague hung up, and he took the next call. A few minutes later, Margaret stormed over.

"Susan told me you wouldn't take a call from a customer."

"But I've dealt with this guy so many times."

"He's a customer."

"He's driving me crazy."

"I listened to the call."

"I've tried to help him––"

"How dare you speak to a colleague like that! How dare you refuse to speak with a customer!"

"But I made an appointment for a reading, and he didn't keep it. I made another appointment––"

"There are too many meter reading appointments booked by people in this team." Margaret's face had gone bright red with anger. "Don't you know it costs this company money every time you make one?"

"But––"

"No buts! Management have decided *all* requests have to come through the

2ICs from now on. And you're going to call Mr Russell back to apologize. You're a customer service officer. *Customer service*. Have you forgotten what that means?"

And she stormed off again before he could add anything more.

Mr Russell, of course, was angry. He blasted Alan about how long it took a bill to be sent, how difficult it was to get through to anybody who knew what they were talking about.

"And I have to go through the same thing again and again with every person I speak to. I'm thinking of calling a current affairs show."

At the end of call, Alan typed a call note into the account:

BILL DELAYED. NOTIFIED BILLING TO ISSUE BILL ASAP. CUNT DISSATISFIED WITH SERVICE AND THREATENING TO NOTIFY MEDIA.

As he was about to save the entry, he noticed the misspelling. He started to backspace to retype the abbreviation for *customer*. And then, he suddenly realized it wouldn't matter at all. No matter what he wrote, no matter how many times he tried to resolve Mr Russell's problem, there would always be something else, somebody else, some other complaint. He pushed a button which would cancel any further calls coming to his phone, took off his headset and laid it on the desk.

Rob gave him a quizzical look as he walked past, but had to return to his own caller and couldn't say anything to him.

\* \* \*

On TV, a cartoon character was trying to hold back the walls that were closing in on him. The villain was cackling gleefully, but the threatened anti-hero was frantic, screaming, making no sense. It was supposed to be funny.

"I could hear the TV down the hall," said Julie, pushing the door open with a plastic bag of shopping. "What are you watching? I thought you hated cartoons."

He made no response.

"Come and help me in the kitchen. I'm making tacos."

Again, no response.

"Alan, I'm speaking to you. Can you turn that thing down?"

"I quit today."

"What do you mean, you quit?"

"Handed in my resignation. I'm gone. Poof!" He brought his fists together, then flung them apart, opening his hands at the same time to indicate an explosion. "It's over. I finish up in a week."

"But you––what will you do?"

He shrugged. "I'll go on unemployment benefits."

"Benefits? No, that'll barely pay your side of the rent and groceries. And if *you've* quit, don't you think they'll start looking at *me*? They know we live together. If we both end up unemployed, how can we afford to live in the city?"

"We don't have to live in the middle of the city. We can go somewhere else, somewhere cheaper."

"Cheaper? Where?"

"I was thinking maybe…Carnegie?" That was where the Russells lived.

She was nonplussed by this sudden change. "Is it the 2IC position?" she asked. "Is that what this is all about? There'll be other positions. You could look at shifting departments. Perhaps the Installations department …"

"Go back and start at the bottom again, you mean?"

"It'd be a change."

"No…It's not that, anyhow."

"Then is it what happened in bed the other night? Don't worry about it––most guys fail once in a while."

"How many times have *you* had a guy fail in bed?"

"I—well, Kylie says it's happened to guys she's been with at least…well, a couple of times."

"Kylie trawls the nightclubs," Alan reminded her. "She picks up guys who are half tanked. No wonder she gets failures. Anyhow, it's just…it's me." He turned back to the TV, where the coyote's plans to demolish the roadrunner had backfired. Again.

"Will you turn off that bloody thing and have a conversation with me?" She picked up the remote control and flicked off the TV. "Margaret was really pissed with you over something today, wasn't she?"

"A customer…" He'd lost count of the number of conversations he'd had with Mr Russell.

"But there will always be bad customers. Once they hang up you get somebody else."

"Yeah, another bad customer. Somebody else who's pissed at something and thinks they'll just take it out on the poor damned customer service rep."

"But that's our job. That's what we do for a living. It might not be the best of jobs, but it pays the rent. It pays for our lifestyle."

He didn't answer, turned back to the blank TV.

"Look…" She paused, gathering her thoughts. "When we moved in here, we knew it wasn't going to be permanent. We knew we'd eventually go further out, have a family maybe. But not *now*, not when all our friends live in the city, not when it's just a five minute walk to work. I'm not ready to commit to a house. I'm not ready to change my lifestyle just because you've had a bad day." He was silent. "You've changed in the past few weeks…I—oh, I can't deal with this right now."

She let the door slam on her way out, and a couple of minutes later the phone in the kitchen rang. He picked up the receiver and held it to his ear.

"Julie?" he asked.

"No, this isn't Julie," said a ragged, old man voice at the other end. "This is Mr Russell."

He dropped the receiver.

* * *

"They're having a sendoff for you," said Rob, crouching by Alan's desk. "You applied for that job with *Prime Energy*, didn't you? You sly dog. Is that why Julie left you? Look, man, I don't wanna get too personal, but…"

There was a beep in Alan's ear, and he held a finger to the headset.

Rob waved a hand to indicate that he was going back to his own desk

Alan barely managed to get through: "Good afternoon, this is Alan. How can I help you?" when an old woman screeched into his ear: "We didn't get the pensioner discount!"

He pulled the earpiece away.

"It's not a discount," he explained, "it's a *concession*. That means the *government* pays part of your bill." Only two more days of this crap left. "I'll need your account number and social security details."

The woman went off to get the information.

Julie hadn't come home, except to pick up some clothes. He saw her at work, but she looked away whenever their eyes met, brushed past if they encountered each other in the coffee room. Rumor around the call center was that she was living with her friend Kylie, and that they'd been partying pretty hard for the past week. He remembered now that the rent was due again next week.

When the old woman came back to the phone, she rattled off her details so quickly that he couldn't even write it down.

"I'll need your electricity account number first."

"It's in my husband's name." Screechy, old-woman voice. "Does it matter?"

"I'll need his social security details rather than yours."

"He's in the garden. You don't mind waiting for a few seconds, do you?"

She went off without waiting for a reply. He watched the seconds, then minutes, pass on his computer screen, considering whether to hang up.

*What does it matter?* he decided. What would it matter if the woman took the rest of the day? What would it matter if Margaret was incensed by his call times? He'd be out of here soon enough.

There was some garbled background conversation on the line as the woman talked to her husband, and then a gruff voice came on the line: "This is Terry Russell. Why in God's name won't you deal with my wife? You people–"

\* \* \*

Margaret and a couple of other girls were preparing food in the lunchroom, and he realized they must have intended having some sort of going-away party for him.

"You're not supposed to be out here," said one of the girls, and another added, "This is supposed to be a surprise."

Alan didn't care. He'd made a snap decision that Margaret and the call center and the customers could all go to hell. He'd never have to deal with the likes of Mr and Mrs Russell again. He'd always thought of Colin and Rob as good friends, but he realized now they were no more than acquaintances at work and a couple of nights a week at the bar. It was a pity about Julie – he'd always thought that she was the stable part of his life – but if he kept her out of his mind for a few seconds more, he'd never have to think about her again, either. He pushed open the balcony door, stepped onto the edge of a potted palm, leaped over the railing without thinking anything more.

There was the sensation of falling, the air gushing past, the ground rushing up and then a thud.

And then nothing.

\* \* \*

"There's an article here about someone jumping off a building in the city," said Mrs Russell.

"Really?" said her husband. He scanned it quickly. *Alan Perry...distraught over a relationship breakdown...resigned from his job...fell six stories...*

There'd been a photo of the boy, but it had been cut from the front page. Mr Russell shifted the scissors out of the way to read more.

He raised his eyebrows. "Not able to cope with life, I'd say. Too soft. Nobody we knew, was it?"

She didn't answer. She was pushing a picture into a frame – a picture of a young man with a company logo on his blue polo shirt – and lifted it to join several other photos of young men and women on a shelf.

Mr Russell waved a sheet of paper in the air. "Now, about this phone bill..."

There was just a hint of evil in his voice.

# 6

## The Tell-Tale Click

**By Tracy Lynn**

Click-click-click.

Click-click-click.

That rhythm, the soundtrack of my day. Always that damn click-click-click.

Never ceasing. Never. Ceasing.

From nine to five she clicks. Red nails tapping absently on black plastic computer keys in that same blasted tempo. In constant movement, she drums during moments of thought or pause. Those damned fingers, painted their perpetual blood red, do not halt for a blasted moment from day's beginning to end. Those cursed nails, sometimes bejeweled and sometimes not, but always clacking on their abused keys, even when not typing. Moving simply out of compulsion and habit, they reign down in an incessant, grating drum of perfect, monotonous rhythm. A cadence that had fallen on my ears each day with the finesse and subtlety of water torture.

Shrouded beyond this meager cubicle wall we share, she sits endlessly rapping at her keys. Always facing me, but never seeing the anguished eyes of her neighbor through the divide.

I'd worked to ignore the other annoyances during those first few months we'd shared this wall, adapting to each nuisance and rising above it. We'd danced that dance for several months. Months in which I'd learned to forgive her overly boisterous phone voice. I'd made my peace with the smells of the Greek food she favored for lunch. I'd managed to ignore her ancient desk lamp with its frayed wire that made it blink whenever jostled. I had even come to terms with the Billy Joel song she played on repeat daily, yet somehow still didn't seem to know the proper words to. I mean for the love of it all, how many times could she mumble the wrong lyrics to that same damn song she listened to every freaking day! How was it even possible that... ARGH!!! And yet... I had made peace with all of these offenses. Each of these grievances I had learned to accept, but it was that click-click-click of drumming acrylic that I simply could not abide.

I'd suffered silently that entire first year, willing myself to be impervious to the drumming. Then, when I could no longer pretend to acclimate, I'd advanced to passive aggressive warfare. Yet no amount of annoyed grunts, loud throat clearing, or increased radio volume would make her stop that maddening drumming. No, something had to be done, and it must be done today! Yes, today was a special day. Today was, in fact, our anniversary of that time when two years prior when I'd eagerly claimed this open desk by the window, overjoyed at my good luck. Two years in which she had drummed the hours away, and in so doing pushed me to this end. Oh yes, today it would end. It had to end. Two years of rhythmic clicks it had been, but there would be not a single day more.

I'd planned for this moment carefully. Each click-click-click had urged me closer to this, my hour of salvation. I felt the sweet anticipation welling inside me as I watched the clock usher me toward the chosen hour when that infernal drumming would cease.

Forever.

I waited until I was sure that she had gone to acquire food, for food was necessary to produce energy, and energy was essential for click-click-clicking. I sat perfectly still and completely unnoticed until all sounds of activity had fallen away and I knew that I was alone.

It was time.

I retrieved my tools and leaped onto my desk, lithe even in heels like a stealth jungle cat. With the steady patience that can only be born of long, agonizing hardship, I lifted my head ever so gradually over the cubicle wall, once more assuring myself of solitude. I was alone; alone in perfect, wonderful, orgasmic silence.

With not a moment to spare I hoisted myself onto the slim cubicle wall, which was no small feat in a pencil skirt and pantyhose. The unstable wall shook, but I remained firm atop my perch staring down at the black plastic keyboard that had so vexed me. The keys were worn in places from so many years of drumming. They looked exhausted, as if they were begging me to put them out of their misery.

I slid over the cubicle in what would have been a perfect dismount had my skirt not caught on the poorly assembled dividing wall. But it was no matter. Nothing would stop me now, not even a rip running from hem to thigh.

I bent over the offending computer, hungry for my victory and short on private minutes. Without further hesitation I produced my only necessary tool. A grin quite sinister spread across my face as I admired the gleaming bottle that would bring about my peaceful, hushed sanity. Never had rubber cement elicited such euphoria in the heart of a person as it did in this moment.

I opened the bottle.

I welcomed the toxic aroma.

My eyes scanned the keys, eagerly choosing which offensive button would be the first to go, and knowing that it would have to be that damn space bar. Oh yes, it would be the first to be silenced.

A maniacal laugh escaped my lips as I slowly brushed the keys with the epoxy, coating each one with a thick layer of muffling rubber. A beautiful, sticky barrier between the hard keys and the ever drumming red plastic talons that played them.

The keyboard glistened when the job was complete, but I wanted more. I craved further satisfaction and I couldn't truly be at peace until the bottle was drained. I tipped it downward, urging the remaining ounces to spill beneath the keys, oozing outward from there and filling the plastic cavity with deadening cement.

It was done. It was done and I was free.

More swiftly than I believed possible I lifted myself back over the cubicle wall and crumpled blissfully into my chair. My timing had been flawless and I sat enjoying the serenity of the empty room, ticking off each moment and knowing my cement was hardening with each tick of the clock. It would be dry by now.

People filtered back to their desks and I listened gleefully as my foe resumed her seat. I waited for the moment of victory.

Three muffled taps, too faint to be objectionable, came from the foiled keys as she tried to drum. Three more muffled taps and my satisfaction grew. Yes, the world had been righted and the drumming had been vanquished. And it was wonderf—

CLICK-CLICK-CLICK.

The ferocious drumming fractured my hard earned serenity. No! It couldn't be.

CLICK-CLICK-CLICK. Determined nails pushed forcefully onto the stubborn keys, urging them to move once again as they had in their prime. Yet they resisted her insistence.

CLICK-CLICK-CLICK. She continued to fight the keys, demanding submission.

CLICK-CLICK-CLICK. My eye began to twitch in syncopation with the growing volume of the drumming.

CLICK-CLICK-CLICK. My body tensed.

CLICK-CLICK-CLICK. My victory faded.

CLICK-CLICK-CLICK. My ire grew.

The drumming matured, growing more powerful and valiantly determined. Those red nails powered through, undeterred by the translucent cement.

CLICK-CLICK-CLICK.

My head ached, throbbing in three-patterned sequence with her clicks. It hadn't worked. The drumming could not be beaten. I couldn't stand this. Not for one more infuriating second. The drumming had won, and I was defeated. There would be no escaping this personal purgatory of synchronized mind games. This was my fate and I felt it like a crushing weight bearing down on my chest. The cubicle was shrinking around me and that blasted desk lamp beyond my wall was blinking rhythmically to the pace of her fervent drumming as the extra force disturbing its frayed wire.

CLICK-CLICK-CLICK.

My brain screamed an enraged litany of: No, no, NO! No more of this damn drumming! I can't take another second. Not one more fucking second!

Except… the words were *not* in just my head. No, they were pouring from my mouth. My lips had taken reigns without my consent, just as my hands had taken unbidden hold of the cubicle wall separating me from my tormentor, shaking vehemently to the same droning rhythm as her drums. Pens flew about and papers littered the ground, but I could no longer be concerned with such things. There was nothing here to me except for that incessant rhythm of cheap acrylic digits on apparently un-jinxable keys.

My hands ceased their assault on the meager wall, falling spent into my lap. My lips, no longer possessed, were now motionless. As motionless as the rest of the room. Not a sound was heard in the entire space. Not a ringing phone, not a clearing throat, and not a blessed damn click-click-click. Not any sound of any form, until my red-clawed foe finally spoke.

"Oh my god, is somebody back there? Hey Albert, did you know somebody worked behind our wall?"

And fucking Albert. "Huh, I guess I always assumed that was storage. Look, I.T. is here with your new keyboard."

Click-click-click.

# PART II

# Nonfiction

*Edited by Brad King*

# 7

# The Worst Teaching Story I Know

## By Chris Huntington

I teach high school, which is only sometimes as horrible as it looks in the movies. Then again, I spent ten years teaching in medium security prisons, so maybe I'm not a good judge. Is teaching a bad job? The worst thing that ever happened to me didn't happen to me, exactly. It happened to a friend of mine. I haven't seen her in years, but I understand she doesn't teach anymore.

The worst thing that ever happened to me?

In prisons, my students sometimes stole from me and often lied; my co-workers sometimes brutalized me too, for that matter. For example: after my wife and I adopted our son from Ethiopia, a fellow teacher joked that the next time, I should save some money and get myself a monkey instead. He'd seen a family on TV that got a chimp and dressed it in little pants and a hat. I heard this kind of thing every day for ten years. It wasn't so bad when you were used to it.

That wasn't the worst part.

In a medium security prison outside Putnamville, Indiana, I had a student named Armando. The black guys in class described him as "long hair, don't care," but he did care. Armando was Mexican by way of Chicago. I managed to bring in a DVD of *The Motorcycle Diaries* and showed it to my students as part of their GED studies. Was it geography? History? For most of my students, it was "reading" because they had never watched a movie with subtitles before. Armando put a chair right in front of the screen, watched the whole thing without talking, then asked me all about Ernesto Guevara and what had happened. He said his uncle had always had a poster of Che on the wall but never explained it. When Armando qualified to take the G.E.D., I called gave him a slip of paper saying he'd passed our pre-test. I expected him to say something, but instead he just held the paper in his hand and stared at the chalkboard. I came back and saw that his eyes were wet. He couldn't turn around because he didn't want the other men to see him crying. "Thanks," he said softly. "I didn't think I'd ever get my G.E.D."

"You will," I said. "You'll take the real test next week. And you'll pass."

He murmured, "Before I met you, I always thought I was stupid . . ."

I felt my own chest tighten, happy, but I frowned. "Hey, wait a minute," I said, "what do you mean by *that?*"

Armando laughed and said *thanks* in that belligerent way we all had in the prison. I told him that when he got his G.E.D. I wanted him to come back and be my clerk; he could tutor the new guys and help me out. He liked that.

But over the next seven days, before he could take the official exam, the prison had a fundraiser. Inmates were allowed to order some KFC, which was carried through the sally port in several dozen plastic bags. Apparently somebody had borrowed money to buy some chicken but didn't pay it back, and Armando, as one of the younger guys in the Mexican crew, was sent to take care of this, and he stabbed another inmate in the neck with a homemade knife. I never saw him again. It made me sad for all the obvious reasons. He was one of my favorite students. The last morning I saw Armando was one of the worst moments in my teaching career just because it was so close to being one of my best.

Early in my career, I worked with "emotionally disturbed" middle school boys and before that, with first graders who had similar problems. I wept in front of two students, little boys, because I was trying so hard. I cared so much, but they were still damaged. I failed. And yet! Maybe they were not as damaged as before. In some ways, it was a harder job than the prison. I had gone into teaching with the attitude that I could change people. Make their lives better. Prisons taught me that sometimes things don't work out.

My co-worker who made the joke about the monkey? He was the first to admit how redneck he was. He didn't *mean anything* by it. He apologized when he saw he'd hurt my feelings, though he didn't really understand why I was upset. In the end, it's just a funny story to me now. I still love that guy. All those inmates who wanted me to give them a break, cheat for them somehow? It's okay. No harm done. I was there for ten years; some guys never got their G.E.D.'s.

Some *did*. I liked Armando, but it didn't work out. That's one thing I learned in prison: it's an imperfect world.

The worst teaching story I've ever heard happened to my friend Himiko. She's the teacher who quit teaching.

Himiko told me that when she'd started teaching Japanese at an American school in Japan, she organized a trip for her middle school classes to visit a traditional Japanese inn in the mountains. The *ryokan* featured communal baths: men on one side, women on the other. The first night, the innkeeper came to Himiko and told her that Himiko's students –all nervous middle school girls—were wrapping themselves in big towels and wearing the towels into the water, laughing so loudly that it was making all the Japanese guests uncomfortable. The innkeeper was embarrassed, but people were complaining. So Himiko had to take a cotton robe and go into the baths and tell the teenagers that this was not acceptable. She told them, loudly, that in Japan, it was *normal* to take a bath in front of strangers and not something to giggle about. Only weirdos made a big deal about being naked in a bath. They just stared at her in their wet towels. And then she felt like she had to put *her money where her mouth was*, and so she got undressed. When a student started giggling, Himiko blurted: "Are you a weirdo? Are you?" She made them put all their wet towels in a pile and start over. All of them naked, such a small room. She laughed when she told the story years later— but at the time, she said, *she just wanted to go home.*

My friend Himiko, when she was starting out —she tried too hard. She didn't have to take off all her clothes to convey Japanese culture. What saved her is that, years later, she could laugh about it. She wasn't traumatized, but she knew she was unsuited to the life. She was a better teacher than me, but she was a perfectionist. She left teaching. You can't be a perfectionist and a teacher both.

At my current school, my students are all teenagers and college bound. "What do I have to offer you?" I ask them. "Everyone in this department knows the curriculum, knows English literature—but I am reasonably sure I know more than anyone else on campus about depriving men of their liberty. Also: failure."

And then I tell I tell them: it's okay to fail. *Life goes on.*

# 8

## Joining the 85% that Don't Survive

### By Thomas Sullivan

The elevator carries me to the top of Seattle's tallest building and lets me out on the 45th floor. I stroll down a corridor lined with art work, push open the heavy oak door at Adams & Associates, and step into a room filled with cubicles and blaring phones. Behind the marble-topped reception desk, I see stressed-out people in business suits scurrying about.

I'm relieved that I've worn my charcoal suit with pinstripes. When interviewing, I always try to match my surroundings. But for a temp agency, I had no idea how to dress. *In clothes I wouldn't be keeping long?* I went with the high-end outfit and got it right.

A receptionist greets me with false enthusiasm. I follow her clacking high heels into a spotless office. Tall, leather-backed chairs surround an antique mahogany desk. Through the ceiling-to-floor windows I see the shipyard cranes south of downtown.

I hear my name and spin around to see a petite woman dressed in an Ann Taylor outfit, her hair coiffed to perfection. It's Kimberley, the owner. We shake hands and grab our seats.

The first stage of any interview is always a strange dance of snap judgments and feigned excitement, where each person tries to gauge the other's worthiness—it's like meeting your teenage daughter's boyfriend for the first time. But I'm well matched for a job teaching computer software to adults.

Kimberley's school is a startup, teaching software applications and basic computer practices like email and web-searches. It will be a subsidiary of the main temp-staffing business. Its customers will be "nontraditional" students: daytime workers who need a night class; seniors learning computing for the first time; unemployed workers retraining for jobs in a different industry. Many will be learning computer apps for temp jobs they get through Adams & Associates.

If this job works out, it'll be the second time I've worked for a private training school. My first involved teaching low-income people in South Seattle who were seeking jobs as secretaries, bookkeepers, etc. Many were hoping to escape difficult backgrounds or bad relationships. The school was expensive to attend, but students were encouraged to get federal loans which, they were told, they could easily pay off after they found work.

I had no idea at the time how easy it was to set up a private college, or how poorly regulated they tended to be. My employer turned out to be a cut-rate operator who used ancient computers, older software, and outdated curriculum. Unwittingly, I became part of a predatory scheme where people, often recruited at Welfare offices or Unemployment bureaus, ended up with few skills but plenty of debt. I left the school soon after a salesman complained to me that he was being pushed to scare students into signing up for our program ("If you don't enroll here, you'll end up having no future.") A year after I slunk away in shame, a group of unemployed graduates and former teachers launched a class action lawsuit. The feds started investigating student loan fraud and the company shut down.

But I'm expecting better results here. Kimberley seems like a sharp operator. She got my name right when we shook hands, unlike the interviewer at the last school, who was holding a half-eaten doughnut in his other hand when we first met. And Kimberley's plans for her new school sound solid.

Kimberley glances down at her watch. She must have somewhere to be, so it's time to finish up the interview. She issues a tight smile and asks one final question.

"Where do you think the school will be a year from now?"

I grin and say, "Right where it's located now?"

I get the job.

* * *

(SIX MONTHS LATER)

Pam bursts into the classroom shortly after our team meeting is slated to begin. Her frizzy hair bounces above her face, which is marred by deep, workaholic wrinkles and baggy eyes. The Staffing Specialists scurry to their cubicles and start calling companies eager to shed labor costs by hiring temps. Pam is the company's #2, just in from downtown. No one wants *anything* getting back to Kimberley, so they do their best to look busy and productive. People summoned to headquarters rarely return. Everyone remembers Jake, our last office manager, who ended up in the Anchorage office, dispatched to our northern gulag with little advance notice.

Pam is like a cross between Vladimir Putin and an ashtray. I can smell her cigarette stench from ten feet away.

The meeting begins with an update from the Sales team. In addition to her many duties downtown, Pam also oversees the sales force at the school. She listens to the feeble results and shakes her head. The two salespeople shift uncomfortably in their seats.

Pam glances at her watch, lurches out of her chair, and marches over to the whiteboard. After drawing two intersecting circles, she starts motivating, Tony Robbins style. We sit and nod silently. The core concept of the lecture is "synergy": multiple bodies working together yield better results than each body operating independently. Like honeybees. Like parts in a car. Like co-workers with far greater concerns nodding their heads in silent despair.

Pam finishes motivating and glances down at her watch. She looks back up at us with a dead expression and says, "So, do we have our ducks in a row now?"

One of the Sales guys, the newer of the pair, chuckles and says, "Since we teach spreadsheets, can we have them in a column instead?"

Pam glares at the guy and his small grin quickly disappears. He's learning what the rest of us already know—you *never* joke with Pam. I doubt he'll be around much longer.

The meeting ends and I stroll to the restroom, thinking that we didn't address the IT roll-out. We're starting a computer networking program next month, and the equipment issues are pressing. We don't have servers, and Pam thinks we can just use regular computers that "look the same but cost less."

As I re-enter the classroom Pam says, "Let's do lunch."

Pam and I drive the two blocks to *Sanfords*, which is tucked between a Jiffy Lube and an Arby's. *Sanfords* is a relic of the 1970's with cheap chandeliers, fake mahogany paneling, and tall menus encased in heavy, plastic binders. It feels like a mob restaurant that has seen better days.

We settle into a padded booth near the back. Pam fires up a skinny cigarette and takes a sustained drag. A moment later she blows out a stream of smoke, exhaling dragon style.

I try making small talk by asking Pam what she has planned for the weekend. Pam flashes a wicked grin. Her pointy, sharp teeth are dark yellow, almost black in places. Pam's mouth could easily be used for one of those scare tactic images they place on cigarette packs in Canada.

"I have to go to the office in Anchorage...I *hate* Anchorage, *especially* in the winter."

A waiter arrives. Pam orders the popcorn shrimp and I get the roast beef sandwich. The fish and chips are tempting, but there's no way I'm getting something deep fried at this place. They probably get their frying oil from the Jiffy Lube next door.

Pam takes a power drag on her cigarette, turns her head sideway, and blows an ash-plume of smoke over her shoulder. Then she turns back and says, "So what's this about Kurt needing computers?"

Kurt, who is the school's IT chief, has been pushing Pam to get the equipment we need. Schools can charge students a lot more for an IT program than a basic computer program, since the jobs (like Network Systems Engineer) that students get after graduating are higher-skilled and pay quite well. But the equipment and teachers needed to do the training right is expensive, which violates Pam's cost cutting and profit maximizing desires. Basically, Pam wants to charge students a lot and train them on the cheap. She and Kurt have now stopped talking, so I've become the go-between.

"Well," I reply, "Kurt needs actual *servers* to do the lessons."

Pam stubs out her cigarette and scrambles to light a second as Rod Stewart comes onto the restaurant's stereo, singing something about "feeling sexy." I'm quickly losing my appetite.

Pam asks, "Can't he just go get one at that place?"

"Yeah, technically, but they're expensive. I know *I* wouldn't want to shell out $1,200."

"That place" is Circuit City, where Kurt buys equipment with his own credit card, submits a receipt to headquarters, and then waits to get reimbursed, which takes months. Apart from Kurt's outstanding credit card bill, our school doesn't have its own budget.

Our food arrives. Pam waves a hand and says, "Go ahead, start…it's okay." She keeps working her cigarette while I fiddle with my water glass, buying time. I can't start eating until the butt is out. It's like having a picnic near the tailpipe of a running car.

Pam crushes out the butt, stabs a shrimp with her fork and moves it towards her open mouth. I feel like I'm watching a shark feed. I turn away.

*    *    *

The school is silent when I return. And empty. I only see Jerry, the Staffing Specialist who places temps into jobs at warehouses and factories. Jerry looks up from his cubicle.

"I have no idea what's up," he says, "but at least it's *quiet* for a change."

I step into the classroom, boot up the computers, and check the afternoon's student roster. It's nearly empty, like usual. A moment later, two students arrive and settle into their workstations. I stare past them into the empty main room. It's strange, everyone being gone at the same time. Even Carol, the office manager, is gone.

Pam blows into the office while barking into a cell phone pressed against her ear. She shouts at Jerry for about a minute before jogging down the aisle to Carol's desk.

I head for the coffee room. Jerry sees me and strolls into the coffee room ahead of me. Meanwhile, Pam is scowling at a computer monitor and swearing.

"Did you know about this?" Jerry says.

"About what?" I respond.

Jerry laughs, puts his hands on his hips and shakes his head.

"Everyone bailed at the same time. Even Carol. Pam just found out from Kimberley. I've seen some strange stuff before, but this takes the cake. This place is *fucked*."

I stare at Jerry. I'm no stranger to turnover, but this is like Jonestown.

Jerry grabs a coffee cup from the counter.

"Pam's on Carol's computer trying to find the client information."

"Okay, Jerry," I say. "I don't understand. What's going on?"

"Well," he says, "Kimberley's mom came out of retirement, got the Staffing Specialists down here to come along, and opened up a temp shop of her own. With *Kimberley's* clients."

I stare at Jerry in disbelief. I've only met Kimberley's mom once, on the day before our school officially opened. We had a small celebration in a dingy banquet room at a nearby hotel and Kimberley's mom dropped by for the occasion. She'd been retired for a year, having spent the previous forty building the business up from scratch before handing it off to her daughter. She was a grizzled, tough-looking senior who rose from humble origins in rural eastern Oregon to build the largest staffing business in the city. During four decades of constant work, I imagine she'd had little time to develop other interests that could keep her going as a retiree. The lady was stone cold and unnerving to be around, like the Grim Reaper. Why a mother would do this to her own daughter makes no sense, but then again, very little around here makes sense. She probably just got bored and wanted back in on all the glamour and action.

I wonder silently what it means for the school. And my job.

Jerry chuckles darkly and says, "Pam and Kimberley are calling the client companies, trying to get them back." He walks towards the door while I try to picture the mayhem that must be raging at headquarters.

Jerry stops with his back facing me and groans.

"This is like *Mommie Dearest*. These people are *completely* fucked."

* * *

Over the next few months, emails arrive exhorting the staff to "remain patient during this difficult period." Kimberley battles her mother with lawyers while our office chews through a string of managers. Each is quickly crushed by the demands of team building and fake optimism in the face of reality. The occasional employee from headquarters visits our office bearing tales of employee departure, much the way a retreating soldier would relate tales of mass desertion on the front. Kurt quits and takes his credit card with him, decimating our budget. The IT program is abandoned, saving potential students from racking up thousands of dollars of debt.

With Pam engaged in 24/7 crisis-management at headquarters, I'm saved from further power-lunches at *Sanfords*. Six months later, the main company implodes and the school dies along with it. Students scatter to other schools to try their luck at the next "educational company."

It's unlikely that we'll be missed.

# 9

# One for Sorrow

### By Madeline McEwen

In a recession, landing a job, any job, is like winning the Lotto, and that's how I felt when the temping agency rang me back in the late 1970's.

"Brilliant! I'll take it. When and where?"

"It's only one day," she said, "So don't get your hopes up. Start today, nine o'clock sharp, at Snotty, Dim, and Screwem, Solicitors, on Main Street."

Okay, so that last part is a lie because this was in England, and the names have been changed to protect their skulduggery.

I was up and out of my fleecy pajamas, showered, and perfect in less time than you can shell and redress a peanut, because England in February is damp and moldy, with ice on the insides of the windows. I dried the rain off my bicycle and headed down the hill, faster than a PopTart from a toaster.

I arrived hot and breathless, padlocked the bike to the railings at the back of the building, slipped on my girl shoes, and dashed around to the front entrance with five minutes to spare. The foyer was massive, marble floored, dotted with Corinthian columns, with high ceilings and a glittering chandelier on that gloomy, gray day.

Miss Battleaxe glared at me from behind a heavy mahogany, highly polished desk.

"You must be the temp."

How did she know?

"Next time, use the side door, this entrance is for clients, only."

I wasn't worried, at this rate there'd never be a next time in any case.

"Name?" she said, pencil poised above a book the size of a family bible, but much, much older.

"Madeline but my friends call me, Maddy."

"I meant," she said peering over her bifocals with the brittle patience reserved for the under sevens, "Your surname."

"McEwen." I spelled it for her to save myself from further embarrassment and prevent further interrogation.

Before too long, I was led like a badly house-trained puppy into a large room full of permanent secretaries, not the political kind, but the gainfully employed kind. The tapping of typewriters ceased, and everyone looked me over, only for a second, barely more than a blink.

"You can sit at Miss Best-Secretary-in-the-World's desk. She's off sick today. You'll be working for Mr. You'll-Regret-You-Ever-Came-Here. That's the 'in-tray.'"

Clearly I was far too stupid to read, 'in-tray,' by myself. How did they expect me to type legal papers in that case? But I kept schtum, even though I didn't in reality because schtum is an American word that I didn't know back then. I got started, working from the top of the pile, before moving on to the dictaphone and voice recorded letters. Boy was I ever glad to stick on those headphones and listen to the droning monotone of my temporary boss rather than the animated gossip of my fellow secretaries.

At lunch time, I waited until everyone else had stopped working and left the room before I did the same. No way was I going to let them think I was a slacker. Taking my squashed sandwiches from my backpack, I headed out to the nearest park, five minutes walk away, to sit on a battered bench, watch the ducks and donate my crusts. Only four and a half more hours to go.

The afternoon swept by quickly, because I was a damned fast typist, if not particularly accurate. I made sure I corrected every error, nobody was going to have cause for complaint and passed my completed work to Miss Only-I-Can-Speak-to-the-Bosses. Fine by me. The secretaries were packing up for the day, touching up their make-up, and clothing their typewriters with typewriter shaped covers. I did the same, the latter not the former. I rummaged in my rucksack playing for time. I needed to be the last to leave, dedicated to the very last minute of busyness.

Miss Only, watched me. What was I doing wrong? What had I missed?

"Big rucksack," she said. "Don't you own a handbag?"

"I do, but I didn't bring it."

"Why?"

This was the most conversation I'd had with anyone all day, apart from the ducks.

"I don't have anything to put in it, so I keep it for best."

She laughed, more of a titter, I'd no idea why?

"If you're ever employed again, you might want to use a comb, or perhaps some lipstick."

She stood by the door, holding it open, ushering me out of the inner sanctum, locking the door. I was summarily dismissed.

I trudged home, uphill, pushing the bike, holding the broken chain in one hand.

When I arrived, I found a message on the answering machine–a new fangled invention which meant people could communicate with you when you weren't there. Imagine that! I listened to Miss Temping Agency.

"They want you there for the rest of the week. Phone me back, and tell me if you want it."

Want it. Of course I wanted it. Who wouldn't want to be paid for sitting in a dry, relatively warm space, with one of those fantastic chairs with wheels on the end of its legs?

I spent the rest of the evening fixing my bike in the sitting room which was slightly less cold than outside. I forgot about the handbag and lipstick until the following morning as I skidded to a halt outside the solicitors' office. Damn. Forgotten my girl shoes. Hoping to avoid Miss Battleaxe, I tiptoed my sneakered feet through the side door, bounded up the imperious, deeply-carpeted staircase three at a time, swerved into the secretaries' room, and hid my shameful footwear under the desk. As long as they remained there all day, maybe I'd be safe. Fortunately, the words, "Dress Code," didn't exist back then over there. Unfortunately, "Inappropriate Attire," did, and much chortling ensued at my expense.

"Planning to run the four-minute-mile, are we Miss Mad."

Oh how amusing. Never heard that one before.

"I do believe Miss Mad wants to beat us all in the rush to perfection."

Ho, ho, hum.

"I love how they coordinate with your rucksack," said the last one with an accent that could have sliced my laces.

I grinned good-naturedly. I could take a joke, or three, even if they were bad ones.

The struggle to reach the end of the week was worth every penny in my pay packet, minus taxes and the Temp Agency cut. Not enough for a new bike, but more than enough to boost my flaggingly unemployed ego. The following weeks were fallow, but just when I was beginning to think I might have to give up hope and sell my body on the soggy streets for medical research into the effects of permanent uselessness, I got another call.

"They want you again," Miss Temp said. "They must like you."

"Really?"

"They asked for you specifically."

I was gobsmacked, so I said nothing.

"Play your cards right, Maddy, and they might offer you a permanent position, although you'll still be at the bottom of the pecking order. I'll be sorry to lose you, but best of luck."

Lucky me, the designated chicken little, I'd take any chicken feed on offer even if I had to scratch it from the dirt. Not that there was any dirt at that office. On the contrary, the place seemed cleaner and shinier and posher than on my previous occasion.

I was surprised to be assigned to the same desk. Perhaps, Miss Best-Secretary-in-the-World was on maternity leave, but I didn't dare ask. Instead, I examined her family portrait on the corner for any signs of a baby-bump. None. Oh well, I'd have to be patient. Presumably some high and mighty type would explain, eventually.

Plodding through the week, with my fingers glued to the keys, I wondered what would happen on Friday? Is that when they'd tell me? I worked on tactics. Should I accept straight away, or play it cool instead? Maybe I should pretend to think it over. Perhaps I should ask about terms and conditions, try and sound intelligent, after all, this was a law firm, contracts were their business.

Friday dragged, but only in my mind. Every time the door opened, I expected to see one of the solicitors, some man in a suit with the power to grant me an income, an annual income. I hoped it wouldn't be Mr. Flirty, who blocked my access to the coffee machine, brushed against my body in the very wide corridor, and wanted to know if I had a boyfriend?

By one minute to five, I was sure I'd expire from fear and excitement in equal measures. The secretaries packed their stuff away, pulled on their coats, and retrieved their umbrellas. I dove for the rucksack scuttling for the remaining seconds on this hallowed ground of employment, but it was no use. Time was up. I had nothing to lose, so in a brief bout of self-assertion, I spoke to Miss Only-I-Can-Speak-to-the-Bosses.

"Do you think I'll be needed next week?"

"Shouldn't think so. Miss Best-Secretary-in-the-World is coming back from Tenerife."

"Oh, I see."

"But don't worry. Next time someone's away, we'll be sure to ask the Temp Agency for you."

"Really? Great. Thanks so much."

"No biggy."

"It is a biggy. Thank you. I'm so glad I managed to fit in with you guys." Although I didn't say, 'guys,' because that would have been considered an insult. The correct word was 'ladies,' but I wasn't an American then.

"I wouldn't say that," she said, as my blood flow began to slow and pool in my mud splattered socks. "You don't exactly 'fit in,' do you?"

"I thought…" What did I think? I had no idea. "But didn't you ask for me specifically because I'm a good typist?"

"Hardly." She laughed, more of a scoff.

"Then why?"

"You're not like the other temps. They're like a squad of marauding magpies with their light-fingers stealing everything that's not nailed down. You're the only girl we've had who hasn't cleaned out the stationary supplies in the desk."

## 10

# Seasoned Teachers

### By Elizabeth Philip

When I asked one of the teachers at the lunch table to pass the salt, the principal of our school whipped out a Morton's container that had been blessed by Monsignor. My simple request ignited a fire inside her and while we ate, she circled us, tossing the grains in our direction. As the salt trickled down my scalp, I discreetly leaned over my leftover pasta and gave my head a good shake. The salt missed the intended target, but I thought it best to keep quiet.

A science teacher mustered up the courage to ask, "Sister, what are you doing?"

My gaze shot in his direction, and I worried it would be the last time I'd see him at school.

"Casting out evil," Sister responded with authority. Her handfuls of salt became larger, and her rosary beads jangled an exorcistic knell with each lap around the table. "Satan is busy at work here." My mind started scrambling for any deeds that might warrant such a cleansing. Nothing came to mind as she slung her devil-be-gone in all directions so as not to miss anyone.

We sat in silence, a cluster of wickedness, kicking each other underneath the table: our code for "that's some bat shit crazy right there." Later, we'd whisper in the hallway between classes, chuckling over the fact we'd all just become seasoned teachers no matter how many years we'd taught. For now, we accepted the ugly truth: Sister felt we were in need of an exorcism before the 7th period bell. Clearly, original sin was not something we could argue against at a Catholic school. We were simply damned from the start and forced to embrace her purification ritual as a gift from above. Personally, I'd have forgone such a gift and settled for a pay raise, but you can't put a price on grace.

On days in which the students acted up more than unusual, I pictured Sister behind a fertilizer spreader, sowing the sacramental salt around the perimeter of the school under the cover of darkness. A snowstorm would give her a little respite because the maintenance crew could take over the purging, and it would look like a normal safety precaution. Whenever I feared that my job may be in jeopardy—no one was exempt from a Christmas or spring break firing—I cast an ear downward and listened for the crunching of salt in the entryway of my classroom: a telltale sign of one's need for redemption.

Besides the blessed salt, the sprinkling of holy water was commonplace. Each classroom came equipped with a plastic bottle to douse the four corners of the room for emergency protection against a parent's wrath or a student's sassy mouth. I once considered mixing the water and the salt for ultimate protection against the dark side but worried I might inadvertently turn the hallway into the Red Sea and drown everyone because I had no idea how to safely wield such power. We learned that Sister kept her stash of holy water in her desk drawer. When she summoned teachers upstairs for either chastising or a swift firing, she whipped out the aspergillum and flung water on our backsides as we left her office. Several times, I suppressed the urge to crumple to the floor and pretend to writhe in pain, while screaming, "I'm melting."

Our principal used the sacred sprinklings for more severe transgressions, but there were thousands of minor misdeeds that earned faculty and staff a good tongue thrashing, like wearing the wrong colored sweater.

"That sweater is putrid," Sister once told a fifth grade teacher. "It makes me sick to my stomach to look at you. Don't ever wear that again."

For the teachers with bunions or plantar fasciitis: "Tennis shoes need to be black, and a doctor's note is mandatory," Sister warned us during a faculty meeting. "If the shoes are any other color, you'll be sent home to change."

After the meeting, a kindergarten teacher leaned over and asked, "Where can I find black tennis shoes?"

"At the nun store," the computer teacher chimed in.

"Can a lay person shop at a nun store?" a math teacher asked.

"Just go over to Hot Topic," I said. "They don't care what you are. And your Goth look will be a big hit with the students."

The kindergarten teacher nodded. "Now there's a bonus."

With Sister's gaze upon us each morning as we reported to school, dressing for work became a group effort. I lined up in front of my family and slowly turned around and around. "Okay, can anyone see a reason why I can't wear this to work? And I mean any reason. Be honest."

My daughter scanned my outfit. "You look frumpy. I think you're good."

"You didn't have to be that honest." I sighed. "But frumpy is good. Frumpiness flies under the radar."

After Sister had us too scared to wear anything fashionable and picking apart teachers' clothing was no longer necessary, she moved onto body shaming. "Your arms are ugly," Sister scolded the librarian, who had started working out at the gym. "Cover them up. I don't want to see that."

And for those teachers with big rumps: "Buy a bigger size. You're not a size six anymore," Sister suggested. And God help anyone who wore the trendy English riding pants and boots. "This is school, not a horse show. Go home and change."

May Crowning, a ceremony in which we adorned Mary and baby Jesus with a crown of flowers, delivered a valuable lesson in hair accessories. Sister stopped my co-worker Mary and I in the office area before the first bell. She pointed to Mary's hair. "What on earth possessed you to wear your hair like that today?"

The word "possessed" made us both flinch, thinking we were sure to get salt in our eyes. Mary reached up and patted her bun, encircled with a small wreath of faux flowers. "Is there something inappropriate about my hair? I . . . I can change the style if you want me to. I'll just run into the bathroom for a minute and—"

"Oh, never mind," Sister said and stomped away.

"What the heck was that about?" Mary whispered.

I shrugged. "I have no idea." Then it struck me. "Holy crap, Mary. She thinks you're crowning yourself, like the May Crowning ceremony this morning."

"Do you honestly think she's that crazy?"

"Mary, how long have you worked here?"

At times a mass shaming was necessary. When the sinners were vast in number or the sin was grievous, Sister called an impromptu school assembly or a surprise faculty meeting. It was as if Lucifer himself had strolled down the halls. One day, word made its way to Sister that the 6th graders were playing the *Charlie Charlie Challenge* on the playground. Equipped with two pencils and a piece of paper, they attempted to summon a Mexican Demon. As an English teacher, I feared Sister might ban all writing utensils to curb the transgression. The students filed into the gym, and I doubted the local grocery store had enough salt on hand for this type of purge. Students were lectured. Prayers were recited. Parents were notified. Priests were called. The school was blessed. And blessed. And blessed again. Charlie never did show, but many of the students Googled Ouji board during their next computer class. Unfortunately, Sister's remonstrance about rousing demonic spirits sparked more interest in the supernatural than any Internet fad. Forget cleanliness; ignorance was next to holiness when a bunch of teenagers were involved, but what did I know?

Unfortunately, Sister believed in the truth—or at least her version of the truth—at all costs, and she spared no one's feelings during her moments of enlightenment. "You have an air about you that's off-putting," she told me while I sat across from her during my plan period. "Nobody likes you."

"Nobody?" Sarcasm worked its way into my throat. "Not even my family?"

"Don't be ridiculous. I didn't mean your family." She leaned in. "But more importantly, we have a grave situation. You've done some inappropriate things here at school."

I had learned long ago that Sister had a flexible relationship with honesty, so I played along despite her unfounded accusations. I put my pen to paper and said, "Wow, inappropriate is a strong word. Why don't you describe a couple of inappropriate things I've said or done, and I'll jot them down. I can't change my behavior if I don't know what I've done wrong."

We sat in silence for a couple of minutes while I drew smiley faces on my notepad. She had nothing but a glare for me, finally announcing, "I think we're done for today."

I gathered my belongings and turned to leave. "Please pray for me, Sister," I tossed over my shoulder before I felt a sprinkling of water on my back.

Honestly, her words stung despite their lack of merit, but nothing she said to me compared to the day a second grader stopped Sister in the hallway. The young girl beamed as she told Sister of an angel who came down from above at her grandmother's funeral and flew her loved one up to heaven.

Never having liked the girl's family, Sister bent down, locked her gaze on the innocent child and said, "Both you and I know that your grandmother didn't go to heaven."

Years later, the girl—still heartbroken and scarred—carried that so-called truth to my middle-school composition class, where she swiftly received an "A."

Whether or not the girl's grandmother went to heaven could never be verified, but we do know that Sister became an unwilling travel buddy to purgatory—or, perhaps, worse. A former teacher, whom Sister had fired, purchased a Nunzilla sparking windup toy. Nunzilla, our Happy Hour mascot, embodied all the degradation and abuse that the faculty and staff endured week after week, year after year. In between rounds of the tabletop game Nun Bowling, Nunzilla marched her way across the table, ruler in hand, and collided with the teachers' beer glasses while sparks flew out of her mouth. We shared our crazy Sister stories and laughed whenever Nunzilla tumbled off the table. It was all fun and games until the former teacher died from an unexpected heart attack.

At his funeral, three teachers gathered to ask the man's mother if Nunzilla could accompany him to the grave. Knowing her son's hatred for our principal, the mother agreed. Right before his burial, a teacher slipped Nunzilla into his suitcoat pocket, where the sister would forever remain buried. Throughout the next school year, each time that Sister grimaced I couldn't help but wonder if the flames of hell were lapping at her habit.

# 11

# Prodigal Remodeler

**By James Figy**

I hated remodeling. All day, crumbs of drywall clump into your hair. Paint stains your jeans so often it's uneconomical to care whether they look clean. The first day on a new job always means demo, tearing down, breaking, removing—and you leave scratched up by fiberglass tub surrounds, by that one nail you pulled where only the head came off and the rest remained to stab your forearm, or by the razor-blade edge of a busted tile slicing through the hefty bag and into your leg.

Remodeling wasn't the best of jobs; it wasn't the worst of jobs. It fell somewhere on the middle of the continuum, drifting closer toward awesome or complete bullshit depending on the day. One day, I'd leave work excited, building a plan of attack for the tile I'd lay tomorrow. The next, I'd go home and say I'd rather drive at high speed into a telephone pole than spackle drywall mud the next morning.

At age four, I began riding to work with dad in a series of rusty trucks and vans. I started working with him full-time at age seventeen, and continued full-time until age twenty-one. Then I went to college to pursue writing, which was the beginning of the end for my construction career. But I continued to swing a hammer twenty to thirty hours a week.

I hated how my thin arms would heat up, muscles straining to lift cabinets or carry lumber or break shit. How we'd demolish entire rooms down to nothing but bones and dust, just to rebuild them. How the saw would kick and many times could've taken my hand. How the sawdust would spray into my mouth.

Important note on eating sawdust: There are many flavors—take your time to savor each one, recognize the differences between a fine oak and cheap pine two-by-four. It's an acquired taste.

* * *

Dad's an anomaly in the construction industry. He has a bachelor's in biology. He reads poetry, loves Mary Oliver. He doesn't drink. He doesn't cuss either—unless, maybe, he's just quoting someone. But my rate of expletives would increase exponentially the further away from him I was on a jobsite. When I ran my own jobs, it got bad.

Once, I primed and painted a small home, laid tile in the kitchen, laundry room, and bathroom. Dad was out of town, serving as a counselor for a church youth convention. The job started all right, but as the newlyweds who wanted to bathe in their home became impatient, the situation grew tense. "Goddamnit," I'd shout when no one was around and some new setback materialized.

When the angry voicemails, the passive-aggressive texts began, I didn't want to be in charge anymore. At that point, I was already tired of remodeling. I was too good for it. I was a college senior, big boss of the student newspaper and unpaid intern extraordinaire. Installing tiny tiles for people who saw me as another construction worker was a waste of my time.

Here in Minnesota, six hundred miles away, when I think about remodeling—what it means, why I miss it now and hated it then—I think about how much I wanted out, wanted something more.

It's not an original story. It's a fiction I've written before, scribbled in notebooks or hammered out on my laptop: Man leaves town, woman leaves man, son leaves father. They all make a clean break. But these stories never come to anything—just caricatures of characters with threadbare plots. I realize why, now that I've left remodeling. Making a clean break is not possible, not even in fiction.

* * *

In the months leading up to college graduation, I expected to be back swinging a hammer in cutoff jean shorts as soon as the cap and gown came off. But I landed a job, despite my English degree.

A week after commencement, I began writing, mostly about remodeling, for an online purveyor of ratings and reviews. In the office, if my butt plopped into the mildly comfortable desk chair at eight thirty each morning, if my eyes strained at a computer screen for eight hours, if I could keep my mouth shut during meetings, everything was golden. No sweat. No paint to scratch off my elbows in the shower. No sawdust to eat.

This job was different from remodeling in so many ways. Yes, I'd chopped lumber and shot nails through one board into another, mixed tile mortar and waited for it to slake, mitred and coped crown molding. But I'd never succumbed to any monotony as arcane and tedious as sitting through meetings about web optimization, meetings about profits, meetings about benefits, and meetings about how we need to schedule fewer meetings.

Now, I not only earned U.S. currency, but also paid time off. I received health insurance and life insurance and gym memberships, and I wondered why they tried so hard to make me like them when I was already committed to this relationship.

Listen, I wanted to say, you don't have to try so hard. Me and remodeling, we're over. I can't say anything bad about this job. No, really: The contract included a non-disparagement clause.

* * *

Dad's work van was once white, long before he owned it. Now it's grayish, with flecks of rust around the fenders, with doors that hang crooked and bargain seat covers to hide the torn upholstery. Even the Jack in the Box head on the antenna looks depressed, its face droopy and faded. My siblings call it the creeper van, to dad's chagrin. It lumbers past, holes in the exhaust farting out carbon monoxide. But seeing as it's as old as I am—meaning, it came into the world around the time Reagan left office—no one can blame it for going downhill.

The last morning I rode with dad in the creeper van, I was off work. My employer gave everyone an extra vacation day for the Fourth of July weekend. Sitting in the creeper van, I imagined how coworkers would celebrate Independence Day: sleeping late, eating pancakes stacked five deep and drowning in syrup, cracking open the first beer of the day at twelve fifteen, quipping, "If it's after noon, you're not an alcoholic." Which would really have their audiences—siblings, in-laws, softball teammates, respectively—rolling in the aisles.

For some reason, I promised dad to spend my vacation day helping. He was sentimental when he asked, saying since I'd be gone soon, he'd like to spend some time together. And the six hundred-some miles between Indianapolis and Mankato would, we both believed, put a damper on reliving the glory days. The extra money would help pay for a moving van. After all, it was a month after the wedding, a month before my wife and I left for Minnesota.

From the driver's seat, dad said, "I'd like to put down some of my experiences in writing." As an afterthought, he tacked on: "As fiction."

I looked in his direction, gave him a nod. Not a vigorous nod, one that would say, Sell your tools and start typing—just moderate nod to tell him, Nice, cool, I'm not asleep. My eyelids sagged, but the hand tools, power saws, half-empty boxes of screws rattled around in back. The van shook as we zoomed north on I-65, from Greenwood through downtown Indianapolis. We were going to a job.

"Like this one time," dad said. "When I was a foreman framing apartments, Bob told the crew he couldn't pay them that week. And these two guys started to walk him down the roof, right to the edge, step by step."

He always tells me story ideas. I'd shrug them off back when I was a seventeen-year-one-old know-nothing, with serious plans to become a rockstar. We'd be wrapped up in coveralls and winter coats on some godforsaken snowy day, riding in a different van with no heat, or a truck with no heat, and he'd go off about an idea he had. His breath would rise out as steam over the frozen commute. Back then, I'd reply, Cool, sounds interesting.

Now that I'm the writer, though, I know he wants feedback. He wants the green light. He's not telling me a story—he's pitching it.

I'd heard this story before. I always pictured him young, carrying his heavy tool belt around the plywood roof three stories above the ground. He had a full head of curly hair and a dark mustache. He'd stay up late to memorize blueprints so that he could keep the crew moving through the humid Hoosier summer.

So I knew how he stepped between Bob and the construction workers, pretended to be aloof, and asked them what was going on. I knew what he thought then: Now they're going to push me off, too. But they didn't.

"They backed away," dad said. "But I really think if I hadn't been there, they would've thrown Bob off that roof." Dad smiled. "Anyway," he said, "I just think that'd make an interesting story."

Not too long after the roof incident, dad got his shit together. He sobered up, met my mom, started a family, got born again. He started his own remodeling business in 1987, a year before I was born. Then they bought their own house. It needed considerable renovation, they knew. But who doesn't want to bring their work home with them?

In a picture from that era, dad holds one-year-old me outside our Greenwood fixer-upper, taking a break from hanging siding, laying shingles. He's wearing an IU basketball shirt, jean shorts, toolbelt. A shirtless toddler, I clutch a thirty-ounce framing hammer, my feet propped on a two-by-six spanning about eight feet between sawhorses. Talk about glory days.

* * *

In graduate school, we talk about craft, about point of view and psychic distance and structure and style and filtering and objects of desire. And things that make your head spin.

Sometimes I think I'm just a simple remodeler attempting to write, bumbling through this odd new world, just one misplaced comma away from being sent home.

After first semester, when I went home for Christmas, dad said I needed to come see his current job. He was running a complete remodel of a historic home in Irvington. So I arrived at the jobsite after a meeting, wearing khakis and a sweater and nice shoes. I thought about shouting, "OSHA," to get everyone riled up. Classic remodeling humor.

To renovate the house, they'd stripped away the plaster and lath boards, taking the walls down to studs. They'd run new wiring and plumbing, then brought in a drywall crew. Besides the large addition on back, the walls were all covered and partly painted by the time I saw. Still, I could picture what lay beneath. Where the wires probably snaked from one stud to the next, based simply on where the outlets were. In the unfinished addition, I knew the entire kitchen layout based on pipes and wires and vents. A stove here, dishwasher there, fridge across the way.

Here's craft that I understand, I thought. Here's something I could take apart and put back together, something I could make beautiful and smooth and useful. The way my professors can dissect a piece of writing and see how it works, hold informed opinions on how it was created and why the writer made certain choices—it's how I feel about remodeling.

At the job, my youngest brother, who's fifteen and acts like it, knelt down, pulling staples to help the flooring guy. Dad said later the kid's his "last ace in the hole." Dad's pushing retirement. He doesn't know how many big jobs, especially big framing jobs, his body can take.

But. He smiled pointing to the rafters in the addition he built, showed me the attached deck out back. He said our middle brother, who works at Hobby Lobby, had been helping, too, and would work again tomorrow.

As we walked the jobsite, I wondered for the first time in a long while: How long until I wind up back here? It's not like it hadn't happened before.

But soon they went to lunch, and I went to Sun King for beer. For Christmas, dad gave me a pocket watch. It had a long silver chain, and the price of ten-dollars printed on its packaging. He called it my employee gift. He used to give me a wrench set or work gloves each Christmas. On the front of the pocket watch, my youngest brother crudely engraved, FIGY Constr. 2015, with my initials. The engraved letters had shifted from silver to orangish. I pressed the button, flipping open the cover. On the inside, it simply said: Retired.

* * *

And here at the end, you should know this: I lied. My remodeling career wasn't one straight, unbroken timeline. I set out towards the west coast with a Volkswagen and a dream, like dad did decades earlier. I lived near Portland, Oregon. A good friend's dad let me stay in his house, and because he was starting a construction company, he offered me a job. We never ended up working, though. So soon enough I took a temporary job at Toys 'R' Us, and played guitar and sang in coffee houses on the weekends. My biggest gig turned out to be playing for one waitress in an empty restaurant, getting paid with two egg rolls. I'd go back to my friend's dad's house and try to book another gig.

The return to Indiana went slowly, and the return to working remodel went slower. I worked temporarily in the spring factory in northern Indiana, until I had to slink back south. To Indianapolis, to home. Because I knew even my father's newest workers earned more than minimum wage.

Here I was, the prodigal remodeler. And dad ran embraced me while I walked down the dirt road to our biblical estate, then slaughtered the fattened calf? Not exactly.

Six months in all I was gone. Now it was spring and work was starting to pick back up, and we rolled and brushed on hues of bright yellow in this cheery suburban addition.

Not long after, dad's then work van—Big Green, he called it—started having issues. When we picked it up after repairs, dad's mechanic asked if I was back for good.

Sure, I said.

The mechanic, a little older than dad, said that was good. "I remember when my oldest left," he said. His son had gone to Nashville, Tennessee, to pursue music. Sons are always pursuing something away from their fathers. The mechanic had relied on his son. He said, "It felt like someone had—I don't know—cut my right arm off."

But the son, he must've felt the phantom pain, too, singing in some honky tonk. Must've missed a wrist or thumb nubbin, at least. No way he made it unscathed.

When you run a circular saw through a board, even as thin as a two-by- four, you have to push straight through. You have to forget about the pencil line, ignore if you get a little off.

Because if you try to twist back, to follow your original trajectory, the blade will bind. The saw will kick, jump back at you, still spinning, metal teeth hungry. It kicks much easier the larger the lumber. Precise, flowing motions are required for cutting two-by-ten rafters our four-by-four posts, which you have to cut halfway through on one side because most saw blades aren't tall enough and then flip over and try to match the cut.

Making a clean cut is rough. You look at the board sawn in two and see divots where you cut too far over the pencil line, edges where you didn't cut enough.

Usually, leaving the board a little off works best. "That's why they call it rough framing," dad says. To make a clean cut, you'll run the saw through once or twice. But always, when you do, you cleave more from both boards than you planned.

# 12

# Temporary Insanity

**By Sara Sullivan**

In the summer of 1997 I kicked myself out of paradise.

It didn't happen right away: it took a series of perfectly reasonable low-paying temp jobs at an array of upstanding businesses throughout a beautiful Southern California beach town to make me realize that my life had turned into a dull meaningless hellhole.

That was the same summer I started subscribing to *The New Yorker* magazine. Ordering a subscription was one of the first things I did after graduating from a small Christian liberal arts college in Santa Barbara in a surge of excitement to be an adult and an aspiring academic. I pounced on every issue when it arrived and pored over the articles while collecting $6.25 an hour at various temp agency jobs all over town.

I didn't go anywhere that summer without a copy of *The New Yorker* with me. When a new issue arrived, I would start at the very beginning and lovingly turn each glossy page. I would even read the listings for all the theater and show openings in the city that I had no hope of attending, savoring the exotic sounds of Bleeker Street, Bowery Ballroom, MOMA, and NoHo while drinking endless free Mountain Dews that a friend with a summer job for PepsiCo dropped off at my house every few days. Considering that my share of the rent for the tiny house I was crammed into was less than two hundred bucks a month, the magazine's annual forty dollar subscription was a real investment and I wanted every column of print to count.

Temp jobs suited me well: I only had enough professional outfits for about ten days of work and an attention span that was even shorter. After four years of deep dreamy talks and small classes on a campus crammed with eucalyptus trees and thoughtful professors, I was spoiled. I had figured out how to ace the educational system after sixteen years of schooling, but the rest of the world was an utter mystery.

At Santa Barbara Bank & Trust, I spent a week manually inputting addresses with one hand and trying not to shoot myself in the head with the other. I was parked in a dusty back room at the downtown branch, so when the boss was out of the room I could pull out my issue and hunker down reading. I entered the addresses about four times faster than they expected and would have been done for the day without my furtive magazine breaks.

Next I spent two weeks at a small law firm transcribing dictation and didn't have time to take *The New Yorker* out of my bag at all. I typed away furiously every hour, spitting out page after page of clean fresh copy about the woman who felt sexually harassed by her boss at The Medicine Shoppe or the customer who had a slip-and-fall case against the Vons supermarket by the Arlington Theater. I was sucked into a world of evil employers and various small tragedies while my sweaty fingers danced over the slippery keys trying to keep up with the documentation of abuse. The lawyer was impressed by my typing volume and offered me a permanent job, which I turned down.

At an orchid farm in Goleta I spent a few days sitting beside a telephone that never rang in a small office trailer. The real action was outside, where a long row of women at wooden tables sorted and plucked long flower stems, sweeping the trimmed bits into square holes cut into the table as they chatted to each other in rapid Spanish. I was bored and wished I could understand their conversation.

Instead I underlined all the words in *The New Yorker* that I didn't know that week and carefully looked them all up on the internet: palimpsest, *Sturm und Drang*, leitmotif. My eventual goal was graduate school for a degree in literature, and I was worried that college had not prepared me well enough. As it turns out, I was right. My future grad school classmates had taken multiple literary theory courses and churned out 100-page senior thesis papers during hours that I had spent going to chapel, singing praise songs at Vespers, and shaking my booty at 18-and-Over Dance Night every Thursday at Zelo's.

My next destination was a software company where I learned that Human Resources is a desolate pit into which you never want to crawl. The building had floor to ceiling windows with a view of the ocean so close the spray practically splattered the glass, but I shared a tiny cubicle with the permanent HR employee and spent the whole day filing under her watchful eye so *The New Yorker* never left my purse. Every morning on the way to the office I picked up a plain bagel with cream cheese, a diet Coke, and two sugar packets to sprinkle directly onto the bagel. I would guzzle the soda and polish off the rest of my breakfast while driving down the 101 and belting out The Verve's "Bittersweet Symphony" on repeat between bites. It was the only moment of the day I felt free.

After a few weeks the big boss, a large woman with aggressively curly hair who had graduated from my college ten years earlier, offered me a permanent job and said it was worth doing HR to stay in Santa Barbara. I didn't believe her. After three weeks of mind-numbing alphabetizing and the first few spasms of carpal tunnel syndrome I moved on.

But my worst job in Santa Barbara wasn't a temp job. At least, it wasn't supposed to be. I successfully applied to be an assistant in a chiropractor's office and started one Monday morning at nine o'clock sharp, as good people do all over the world every day. The job was for $10.00 an hour, a major increase over my temp job rate, and it seemed like a good time to settle down and get serious. The very nice older woman who owned the practice spent the entire morning on my orientation: down to which stapler to use for which form and what time the three plants in the atrium needed to be watered with the plastic measuring cup hung on the wall specially for that purpose.

Afterwards I sat myself silently at the smooth receptionist's desk and listened to a clock ticking on the far side of the room. The water cooler made a burble. When my lunch break came, I stumbled into the bright sun of the parking lot and headed for my car in a daze. I drove up to my old college, where my boyfriend was working in the IT department for the summer. As I wound my way through the shady roads of Montecito, I knew I wasn't going back after lunch.

The despair gurgled up into my mouth as I found my boyfriend in the library basement. I couldn't really speak, but the horror of my morning must have been clear enough on my face. Ryan said he would handle it. He called up the nice woman and explained that it had come to his attention that perhaps she had hired a family member of his named Sara Sullivan? Yes, he was very sorry but had to explain that, although from time to time she would in fact pursue employment, Sara Sullivan unfortunately was not in any condition to take a job. Sara Sullivan was in fact recommended against taking up any form of paid labor by her medical caregivers. It was a virtuoso performance: he said exactly all the right, delicate things you would say if your sister or cousin or niece were batshit crazy and a borderline danger to herself.

As he spoke, the dull, heavy weight that had been settling deeper and heavier around my lungs and heart since nine o'clock that morning lifted, and with relief I took a full, free breath again. I realized he was so convincing on the phone because he wasn't lying. Being at a small, well-kept office in an industrial office park all morning had in fact made me a little crazy. I was in no condition to take that job.

Instead I wanted Bleeker Street and gritty subways and the big wide world and meatball subs and to sleep whenever I wanted. And for people to think I was smart, and do work that mattered, and use words like bildungsroman in a sentence. I realized I would have to leave for that. I couldn't stay in beautiful, idyllic, organized Santa Barbara without giving up too much, sinking into a permanent place of compromise and mediocrity. So I decided to move to the East Coast.

During my last few days in town, I ran into the nice chiropractor while I was reading *The New Yorker* and waiting for a sandwich at the takeout counter of a pristine delicatessen downtown. She looked me in the eye with a gentle smile, patted my shoulder, and said softly with utter kindness, "How are you," knowing the answer was not well, but she was too polite not to ask anyway.

# 13

## Mission: Failed

### By Nancy Matson

As soon as you perform five minutes of work doing something you'd never do for free, you understand that the dream job, like Santa, the manic pixie dream girl, and a zero calorie snack that does not create intestinal distress, is a lie. Even if you pursued the job you have thinking it would bring you great personal satisfaction, the day will come when passion and commerce disentangle like the strands of a hand–knitted scarf that's a bit too artisanal to make it through the whole winter season and you are forced to choose only one path, and you will choose the one that leads to a paycheck. It's the afternoon Ryan Gosling's massage therapist grits her teeth through another of his boring cat stories while she works a knot out of his shoulder. It's the evening when the head of Godiva's quality control unit looks out over the vats of chocolate after the other factory workers have gone home and weeps, feeling in his lab coat pocket for an apple, a piece of cheese, anything but another confection.

How do I know? In the mid 1990s, I got paid to play videogames.

When I was 26 and hired by Activision's test department, I did not consider myself to be a gamer per se. I'd logged in hundreds of hours with my Atari 2600 in high school and played casually in the intervening years, but videogames were not an active hobby. Nonetheless, videogames did fall under the umbrella of multimedia, a catchall term common the mid-90s to describe all sorts of burgeoning technologies and the field that inspired my move a year and half prior from New York to Los Angeles.

I was happy to get the job, though my first few days in my new position were bumpy ones. I wasn't delusional enough to think my every whim would be catered to in my new job, and that I'd be benched until the company developed a project featuring a sassy, vintage-jewelry wearing detective/ historian protagonist who investigates Nazi war crimes while eating the occasional chocolate pudding. Still, I figured I'd be given something marginally appropriate to my demographic. A strategy title, perhaps. A light adventure game. Thus, I was not pleased to find out that my first assignment was Mech Warrior, where I assumed the role of a big old robot trying to destroy another big old robot in an arena full of screaming fans.

It wasn't the English version, either. It was the German one. What a great chance to practice my German! Is what I might have thought if I actually spoke German.

"Is there a translation for any of this, by any chance?" I asked Davia, one of the leads. It was only by trial and error that I was able to get the game started. Kottenfire? Kattenfire? Were these even real words?

"Nope," she said, breezing past me to deal with what she considered a real problem.

When I walked into that open air to battle my robot rival, my metal casing glinting in the sun, I knew I didn't stand a chance. I toggled between incomprehensible weapon choices and kept hitting the fire button until, in short order, I was backed into the corner and destroyed. Over and over again.

I did learn two words of German which I retain to this day: mission fehlgeschlagen.

Mission failed.

The main problem with my new job was neither my lack of skill as a robot killer or my limited language skills. It was the size of the paychecks.

We started at $10/hour, no benefits. I could have scraped by on this, despite my outstanding student loans, were it not for a professional setback some weeks prior. I had been laid off from "edutainment" startup Viridis in a group meeting in which they announced they could not make payroll, an especially painful event since they paid us on a monthly basis. Looking back, Viridis' failure seemed inevitable. Their products included such ill-advised titles as Safety Monkey, which starred a poorly animated primate which lectured kids on how to avoid household accidents. His list of tips included, improbably, given that its target audience was first-graders, proper gun storage and were accompanied by his Orwellian catchphrase, "to obey is the way," which inspired us to refer to the game internally as 'Fascist Monkey.' The company's flagship title, Zelda's Adventure, could not play both sound effects and music at the same time and featured such cumbersome loading times that it was panned as "practically unplayable." Even so, our employer's abrupt meltdown came as a shock to me, my co-workers, and Sallie Mae. When I learned there was a way to supplement our regular paychecks, I jumped on it.

Activision offered bonus periods right before the games were due to ship. We receive an extra $500 for working 80 hours a week for several weeks in a row in addition to our hourly wage.

It was ridiculous what sacrifices my fellow testers and I would make to get that money. We'd sleep under their desks, stop showering, miss anniversaries. With every day that passed, the poor time management skills of the average twentysomething gamer were highlighted a little more as shifts became longer and hygiene standards plunged, until schedules defied common sense, logic, and in cases where a public school math education had failed, the space/time continuum. No one wanted to be stuck an hour or two shy of the needed total when the bonus period slammed to a halt.

Luckily for me, a bonus period would be coming up quite soon. I wasn't intimidated by the prospect of an extended schedule. How hard could it be to play videogames for a few extra hours a day?

I was especially bullish about the idea once I was mercifully taken off Mech Warrior and assigned to a modern update of the classic game Pitfall, the original version of which had been released on my old friend, the Atari 2600. No longer was I relegated to an incomprehensible world of harsh-sounding words, facing certain death dozens of times a day. I was fighting my way through a South American jungle as Harry in Pitfall: The Mayan Adventure for Windows 95, whipping monkeys and snakes, picking up gold coins and zipping around on vines, in the adventurousness yet culturally insensitive tradition of Indiana Jones, getting paid for it all the while. I bragged about my new gig to everyone I thought would be impressed. While my contemporaries flooded their alumni newsletters with notices of their United Nations posts, Peace Corps stints and prestigious journal publications for their colleagues, former schoolmates, and distant relatives to admire, I was limited to a more targeted audience: middle school boys.

In reduced circumstances, your dreams become smaller. Being asked to join a presidential cabinet, named a Rhodes Scholar, or even having an angry letter to the editor published in my local free paper were goals that so exceeded the reality of my daily life I could not even fantasize about them. Instead, my daydreams centered on being at a friend's party, cornering one of their kids playing a game I knew intimately, and turning into a sort of James Bond for tweens.

"That boss is tough," I would imagine myself saying, leaning into the kid's bedroom door. Possibly while holding a martini. "You should try the bow and arrow."

The kid would make a dismissive noise, annoyed at some dumb adult's input, his voice infused with as much contempt as you'd feel comfortable directing toward an adult. "I tried it already."

"Oh, really?" I shake my head, amused. "Move over," I'd say. "Let me show you how it's done. I understand you just had a birthday. Maybe a wager to make it interesting?"

In reality, my overtures were both less organic and less well-received. "You like videogames?" I asked the boy my friend babysat for one time.

"Yeah," he said, as if it were a dumb question.

"I get paid to play them," I'd say. "That's my job."

"Really?" he said, half impressed and half disbelieving. I almost told him my hourly wage, as, again, he was at an age that ten bucks an hour probably sounded pretty good, but that was below even me.

While I was pleased to be reassigned to Pitfall, not every tester in my department was so fortunate. As I'd already learned by my time on Mech Warrior, one of the downsides of testing is that you don't get to choose the game you test. If you were told to play Bunny Killer 5, you slaughtered fluffy little rodents for weeks on end. If you were assigned to Fantasy Prom Night, you spent a month choosing accessories, changing the color of your date's hair, and weighing and counterweighing the environmental damage versus the sheer awesomeness of heading off to prom in a Hummer stretch limo. And if you were sick of it? Imagine how sick of it you'd be once you'd tested it in Spanish and French for both Sega and Nintendo.

As we bumped up against the bonus period, everyone in test agreed what getting the short straw meant. "Anything but Atari Action Pack," one of the veteran testers, Rawson, commented. We all nodded in unison. If I didn't think it would have made me look crazy, I would have crossed myself and invoked the Holy Trinity to punctuate his point.

Atari Action Pack was a compilation of emulated versions of games from the 2600 made playable for Windows 95, essentially unchanged from their slightly post-Pong glory. As I said, I had a great fondness for the Atari 2600, and those were fun games at the time – the way a cardboard box is fun when you're two. Most consisted of nothing but a handful of pixels moving from one side of the screen to other implying, but not really showing, a simple sport or task, like fishing or boxing. The original system was equipped with a mere 128 bytes of RAM – I'm not even 100% sure it could display the color orange. Forcing someone to test Atari Action Pack for weeks on end was the videogame equivalent of the U.S. government siege on Manuel Noreiga, when they blasted Guns N' Roses and Jethro Tull at deafening levels outside the embassy of the Holy See embassy, an act which was meant to flush him out to surrender but which also served as arena rock aversion therapy.

After the test period had ended, Rawson recalled that he'd seen Paul, a new tester whose name I did not yet know, testing Action Pack. While most testers' spirits would be quickly crushed by the tedium of a few jaggedy pixels moving back and forth across their screens, shifting in their seats miserably, taking frequent breaks, and complaining to anyone who would listen, Paul never lost his focus. "I saw him play Atari tennis for four hours one time," he told me later, his voice a mixture of fear and awe. "He didn't even get up to go to the bathroom."

I first encountered Paul on the cusp of the bonus period.

We weren't assigned desks, so where we sat varied, depending on what platform we were testing. I plunked down next to him and said hello. At that point, he was no different to me than every other guy – and they were mostly guys – in test. It was an inconspicuous bunch, a little less athletic, a little nerdier than the rest of their age cohort, but otherwise unnotable. They all vanquished enemies, cried out in frustration, and navigated through fantastic worlds in much the same fashion. Still, there was something different about Paul.

"Hello," he said in response to my greeting, pivoting his neck in a strangely non-fluid motion, as if he weren't swiveling his own body but moving the head of a doll. His eyes did not regard me with friendliness, interest, or even suspicion, or any of the other expected responses, but were all pupils, like a portal to another world. Not a fun world, either, like Narnia, or the campus of Hogwarts, but like that part of Middle Earth where the Orcs hung out, or the Matrix, back when everyone's bodies were stuck in oppressive pods and used as an energy source. As he turned toward me, I felt something akin to fear, like the protagonist in a horror movie who discovers that her neighbor has turned into a vampire and has to go from asking to borrow a cup of sugar to driving a stake through the guy's heart.

I muttered something about my computer acting buggy and fled to another workstation. Before my exit, I think I actually banged my hand on the side of the computer, like it was a TV that wasn't coming in right, and I was one of the Three Stooges. In retrospect, I think my lack of acting chops were partly responsible for the problems that followed, probably alerting him that something was wrong, but what was I, a member of the Royal Shakespeare Company?

I chose another station, and fired up my beloved Pitfall. I breezed through the Yaxchilan Lagoon, picking up the hot pepper for additional speed. I blew through the Palenque Ruins, whipping a skeleton midair, a motion as automated as brushing my hair. I picked up every bonus, every life I'd never need, with as much interest as a billionaire finding a ten in an old pair of pants. I took down bosses efficiently and without pleasure, like the hired killer I basically was. Something had changed. I was no longer having fun. I was like a professional skier compelled to repeat the bunny slope, over and over again.

There's something profoundly perverse about doing something for money that most people only do for pleasure. As David Lee Roth or someone who might as well be David Lee Roth once said, after a while, you get tired of having sex with the same Playboy centerfold over and over again.

My growing boredom wasn't my only problem. A few days later our supervisor, Dave, took me aside in the break room.

"Nancy," he said, shutting the door behind us and leaning against the counter, "have you been talking about Paul?"

Paul? Atari Action Pack Paul? I shook my head.

Dave shifted his weight from one leg to the other, looking none too pleased to be fulfilling his managerial duties. "He said you told the other tester 'be careful, he's on to us.'" I reeled from the shock of this.

Sometimes someone repeats something to you that they claim you've said and you don't quite believe it, but you can't rule it out altogether, either. Really? I told you I liked Braveheart? I stated in a drunken stupor that Donald Trump "cleaned up pretty good"? I guess it's not impossible. You're skeptical, but doubt creeps in.

There are other times when doubt does not enter into it.

"I never said that," I said. "I didn't even know his name until this morning." I blubbered on, saying the same things over and over again, until Dave cut me off and sent me back to work. Part of me was worried he didn't believe me. The other part was stressed out that I was wasting non–billable time.

I'm sure Dave was as baffled as I was. He'd brought Paul over from a test department at another company, where he'd presumably not said a series of improbably paranoid things. What had happened since then? Was he mentally ill and off his meds? Was he hallucinating because of sleep deprivation? I had no idea.

I returned to my desk and unpaused Pitfall, shaken. I let go of my bungee cord too early and fell to my death – a total rookie mistake.

Next to me, a tester wrote out a series of numbers on a pad of paper. "If I work a 20-hour shift on Friday," he explained to everyone within earshot, "I can still take Saturday off for my sister's wedding."

By the last week of the bonus period, everyone was showing the strain. Testers fielded angry phone calls from the girlfriends they were ignoring. The air was fetid with the smell of sweat and unwashed feet. Those who had fallen badly behind were reluctant to leave for lunch, reduced to eating whatever was on hand to keep themselves going. Many a meal was fashioned out of whatever was available from the closest vending machine.

I was suffering from the existential crisis that befalls every adult spending all their conscious hours playing videogames. Is this what I should be doing with my life? Was this the truest expression of my highest self? Was it too late for me to go to law school? I had entered a weird zone where a task required my complete attention and yet my mind rebelled the whole time. It reminded me of when I got detention in the seventh grade and the teacher made us stare at a chalk X he'd drawn on the board for the entire hour and parts of the letter began disappearing as the minutes dragged on, like my very eyes shut down in protest.

I recognized my situation wasn't objectively that bad. I wasn't a damn coal miner. Nonetheless, like a petulant rich child who has grown tired of her view from the backseat of a Rolls Royce and who only takes pleasure at pelting innocent passerby with Faberge eggs, my attention, along with my goals, shifted. My goal became not to play the game well, but to crash it. Where I once basked in the love of gaming, I now took all my boredom and frustration and poured it into a game than I now disdained. We were writing up bugs all along, of course, but now it was my only pleasure.

I was not alone. Our conversations in test now went something like this:

"Aha!" I would yell out, triumphant. "If I hold down all the buttons when I pick up the second ring in Jaina Island Falls, the screen goes black."

"Nice one," said Kenny, another veteran tester, whipping a scorpion with one hand while eating a bag of chips with the other. "If you crawl under this part of the temple in the Lost City of Copan while you throw the boomerang," he said, as we leaned in to observe, "you get stuck. You have to reboot the whole system."

We did things no normal person would ever do to make the games crash. We had Harry crawl under every opening, use every weapon in every situation, whip things that couldn't be whipped, try to push Harry to the edge of death without succumbing. It was our job to be a pain in the ass, and when we succeeded, it was the only thing to break the tedium.

While technically the production team and the testers all had the same goal – to release a successful game with as few bugs as possible – the relationship between us sometimes became contentious, especially as the ship date drew near. Every new bug report was more bad news for them, and they were more exhausted than us. The programmers and producers had been in crunch mode for months trying to make the upcoming deadline.

We would have felt sorry for them if we didn't feel so sorry for ourselves.

A few days later, as the bonus period came down to the wire, I came into work and found out that Rawson and Kenny had been working until around 2 a.m. the previous night, desperate to catch up on their hours, when two L.A.P.D. officers arrived, Paul in tow.

"Your co-worker reports that this man has been badgered and threatened throughout the day by Nancy Matson and Jimmy Murphy," one of the officers said. "Do you know these individuals?"

"Yeah," said Rawson, a bit stunned. "They both work here."

The officer nodded. "Paul told us that Nancy walked by his desk after dinner and said 'I'm going to get you, you fag,'" the officer read off his pad. "He also said Jimmy threatened to wait in the parking lot for him until he got off work because he 'knows what he is.'"

I can only imagine the muted, confused responses of my coworkers as they processed these words. Did they pause their games while they answered? Did they sacrifice electronic lives, not responding to attacks by bosses or other enemies as they answered the officers' questions?

Rawson told me later that they'd defended us, noting that I hadn't even been at work since dinner. Jimmy, who was still there, showed up shortly after they arrived, protesting his own innocence. The cops gradually realized something was amiss, gave up on their inquiry, and, at Paul's request, begrudgingly agreed to walk him to his car. What Jimmy and I had done to him might have been imagined, but his fear was real. After that incident, ours was, too.

I'm not sure if Dave or Human Resources intervened, but Paul didn't show up the next day. Sometime in the early afternoon, we noticed someone else was missing: Jimmy. We hadn't seen him in several hours.

"It doesn't make sense," said Rawson. "I know he needs his hours. Where could he be?" We half-jokingly constructed our plan if Paul were to show up with a weapon while I flipped through the pages of bugs we still had to recheck. If the bugs occurred in the earlier levels, it was easy enough. Fly through a level or two, repeat the action, and see how it went. If the problem had occurred deep into the game, it was a lot worse. There were no shortcuts to get to where you were going. You had to play your way through every previous level, averting enemies, completing every puzzle, sometimes over and over again to get to the site of the reported error. Finding a repeatable bug in the Lost City of Copan? No big deal. The Runaway Minecar level? More annoying. The end boss? Borderline cruel. It was like Sisyphus with pixels.

Though our fear was real, no one considered leaving the building, or taking a day or two off. To abort the bonus period was unthinkable. Hell, none of us even moved our hands away from the keyboard. The sounds of the whip, the tinny music, the restarting. Somewhere in the test room, the death song for Harry from Pitfall played. No big deal. There were plenty more lives where that came from.

Did we all need the money that bad? I sometimes wonder if once you've accepted the premise that you need a job to survive that your work-related decision process is permanently impaired. The truly poor have few other options. For us, hovering somewhere above the bottom of the economic ladder, most with resources to save us from homelessness and starvation if we lost our jobs, was pursuing this bonus period at the possible expense of our personal safety worth it? Or were we all hampered by our wage-related tunnel vision? It was one thing to be bored by the rhythmic pattern of hopping from vine to vine in a pixelated universe. It was another to continue playing knowing your job might now be somewhere on the danger scale between asbestos remover and bush pilot.

No one suggested we stop. For a few hours, no one even suggested we look for Jimmy. We were so close, and we really needed the hours.

Eventually someone found him in the garage. He'd meant to take a short nap in his car to keep himself going, but it had lasted hours. We were relieved and sympathetic. We were glad he hadn't been murdered, obviously, but that wasn't the only reason we worried about him. It wasn't going to be easy to make up those hours.

I ended up successfully completing the bonus period, along with Kenny and Rawson, and reaped my reward in the form of $500 before taxes. The additional income temporarily put us in a higher tax bracket, so our take home percentage was worse than expected. I remember when one of the testers, Chris, opened his check and made a disgusted noise. "I could have just stayed home and jerked off the whole time."

Not long after the bonus period receded, everyone reverted to their old habits. They'd stay late, often many hours late, playing Doom, then Quake, which had seized the imagination of gamers everywhere with its innovative first person shooter design, even though they'd already spent the entire day playing another game on company time. They didn't want to miss the chance to play with each other over the network, which was still a novelty back then. I always declined their offers to join them. I wasn't a true believer like they were. For them, this was as good as it was ever going to get, and it was pretty damn good.

I spent a few years at Activision, moving over to the production side before transitioning to the then nascent dot com industry.

Shortly after that, Activision ceased bonus periods altogether. They hired more employees who worked different shifts, so no one was required to work crazy hours anymore. It became the hugely successful corporation it is today.

Years later I found out what had happened with Paul. Kenny had heard the story from Dave, I think, and he'd passed it on to me. Paul had taken meth during the bonus period to stay awake. He was just trying to make his hours, just like us.

If you ever come across a copy of Earthworm Jim 2, circa 1995, and type in 'paidtoplaygames,' you will access a little known Easter Egg that the producer stuck in. You'll see a photo of everyone who tested it before it went to market, including me.

I haven't seen it in twenty years, but I'm sure we look exhausted.

# PART III

# Poetry

*Edited by Jessica Dyer*

# 14

# Only Son Maimed by Future while Walking Fire Route at Lynch Road Assembly

### By Matt Mullins

He swears this is only temporary, his slipping through the Bakelite darkness, a walkie-talkie and a punch key time clock bouncing against his uniformed hip bones as he paces off the third shift fire route in Lynch Road Assembly where another accident has the lines down indefinitely for inspection. Shadowy, greased machines, mechanized claws, arms and maws with stalled conveyer tongues: all drip viscous rainbows in the yellow beam of the six cell Mag-lite he sweeps across the vacant sockets of headlamp housings and quarter panels, the gap-toothed snarl of grilles. He is the black sheep, the errant college kid, an auto executive's son playing at plant security guard instead of reaching for a white collar beyond this factory he imagines alive again with disassembled parts rolling through loud, pneumatic hours.

During the Second World War, women built diffuser tanks here to distill the radioactive gas now setting his nights aglow with the echo of split atmospheres and the screech of the long drawn second when the assembly line ground up that second shifter's arm to the elbow. He sees the synchronicities in his assignments to posts with sinister pasts: his life as of late in a buckshot spackled guardhouse where he watches the chained gates just beyond the bull-horned prongs of a hi-lo. What is he but a vacation relief bounced from plant to plant, memorizing patrol routes and walkie-talkie call signs? A lost kid ticking the full-timer's grim stories through the half of his mind that isn't on his girlfriend, his buddies out closing the Woodward bars, everybody rolling high and loud into the after hours.

*Young. Not much older than you*, the shift commander had said. *Forgot rule #1: Never look away from the machine.* Staring at it caught in his beam, that *can't* be gristle or blood greasing the gears. It must have been cleaned by now. From what he's heard, the line didn't even hiccup, just kept rolling, stamping out quarter panels until someone hit a kill switch. Now the dead factory throbs with ghost limbed absences. His Mag-lite smears the black, finds the red eye of the assembly line's START button as he wonders what it would be like to see such things rattle back to life. And then what to feed them.

## 15

# Only Son Deconstructs Guilty Shadows of Sexless Angels while Applying for Unemployment upon Graduating College

### By Matt Mullins

*On the dole* his Irish, Catholic grandmother used to call it. Something for the crippled, the nervous, the Sterno bums in rags. Even her so called "sheeny" who rolled his peddler's cart down the alleyways of her childhood to the mantra of *Knives sharpened. Pots mended* had the wherewithal to refuse.

But Only Son, he'd thank God she's dead and blind to what he's come to but for the notion she's clucking that tongue of hers, wagging down from Heaven a bone-finger, the very one she used to ream him out, unplug his constipation the same way she hooked the guts from the holiday bird when he was five and obviously old enough to remember.

You see, Only Son knows nothing about the beaten air held by these men hacking wet downturns of economy into cracked palms, their trying and failing to get beyond the same pounding fist of thought that had set verbal dishes jumping above the dinner table if one dared question the fact that the poor are only poor because they're lazy.

And now he's the one scratching out blunt forms, trying not to read too much into the character flaws implied by such a narrow life's appraisal: *U. S. Ctzn?* (sic) Yes. *Hgh Schl Grad? (sic) Yes. College Grad?* (sic) Yes. *Reason For Inability To Find Work?*

(sic).… And cringing in the shadows of sexless angels he feels her pointed aspersions. Blasphemer. Malingerer. Fornicator. Eternal boy-man with a book and a beer, loafing in a hammock listening to wind stir warm secrets through the leaves as songbirds seem to make verities of all human mystery. A love for ease that aches through yet still allows him to believe that one day he really will bag his possessions for Salvation Armies and go build homes in a Third World.

Instead he turns in the irony of his smudged form. Walks out through the glass doors. A cold robot ballet he performs to the mantra of *Jesus, stop being so guilty of all this. It's not your fault no one's hiring.* Or is it?

Unlocking his car in the parking lot beneath a needling rain, he is pinned to the need to come clean. Be honest. She was less a table pounder and more a sweet old lady singing off-key in her dementia, the one who couldn't remember his name as he, still in college then, danced the whole of her light as a bag of wren bones around his parents' porch.

He longs to be that way, to not remember who you were as you live inside the fading echo of who you are now. That is how we step from the dark to forgive ourselves, to become works in progress, un-judged, incomplete. So radiant as to defy every shadow we cast.

# 16

## Unbelievably Happy Ending

### By Nate Logan

It has been a long day and I require nourishment. I require tiny burgers (no pickles) and sticks of mozzarella. I also require a vanilla shake. I'm sitting in my modest SUV, relaying my needs to the disembodied voice of an angel. This is a miracle that's been with us since 1947. My personal miracle costs five dollars and change.

I pull up to the second window. The crackly, far-away voice now has a body, face, and hairnet. I don't know if she is too young to be in the business of wonder, of appearing on toast. I ask her how her night is going. "It'll be better when I'm off. One more hour," she says. And when she hands me the greasy bag, our fingers briefly touch. Something divine enters my life for which I have no name.

# 17

## Pillow Dictionary

### By Cathleen Allyn Conway

*"Being a lover is close to being a worker."* – *Rumi*

With stacks of page proofs I will build us a bed
between our desks: a mattress made of office supplies,
stuffed with rubber bands and styrofoam peanuts,
blankets knit from packing twine.

Let's crawl inside.
I'll draw the curtains of meshed paper clips
and by the light of our mobile phones we'll
read passages from our favourite style guides:
*Chicago Manual* for me, *Hart's Rules* for you.

Heads on Chambers and the OED, we'll lie
side by side, parentheses, sharing words we dislike.
We'll put the speech marks wherever we want,

mark each other all over in red, English
tongues licking nouns; dialects, couplets,
our iambic beats quickening.

# 18

# Me and Another Girl Work Second Shift at Motto Mart Gas Station

### By Susan Yount

Incidentally, her name was Heather.
My name          everyone knew.

It was southern Indiana after all     *I grew up there*
but Heather didn't.

All our friends got [ ] & [ ] & free ice.   The [ ]
boys left extra.                    We kept          the bathrooms

still looked before we turned on     the pump.

That was the summer      he      was much older.

Attractive                    *blowingsmoke...*

We each had
an ashtray. Cash register. Gas pumps.
Lottery ticket dispenser. Candy bars.

Burned up hotdogs picked up by a homeless man.

Heather had          a husband I had two jobs
thin legs, hair, [ ]     regulars would
see me at the diner first.          He was regular

but not from town.          *Smokyblonde,* kind
you'd like to          fuck offered
two week's wage.          I looked over

cigarette cartons lined up overhead          Heather
flicked–at          an ashtray
caressed the cash register                   [  ]

# 19

# Socks on Fire

**By Susan Yount**

Never mind that the manager instructed you to wear solid black or navy socks. *Hey little pistol.* You'll even forget the four fat fucks at table five. *Want to make some extra cash?* You got the round table tonight and in these smokin' socks you'll serve chicken fried chicken, mashed potatoes and sawmill gravy scintillatingly. *Let me be your pepper, you salty centerfold.* You. The star of the Cracker Barrel Ballet and Roadside Freak Show. Your Glowing Charcoal Argyle Socks (No. 555), dyed in China, will stay mid-calf as you dance to the tune of cranky, deep fried okra. *What time you get off? I'm staying at the hotel next door.* Even that 50-cent tip left by the two old crones is no match for these swanky Uzbekistan-combustible-cotton, hand quilted socks. *Another cup of coffee hon.* Your patrons will be amazed as you blaze through kitchen grease seizing oversized portions of mac and cheese for their delight. *More cornbread. More biscuits.* Then, sparks flickering from your ankles— the manager notices your defiance. You are fired. You're secretly thrilled. He calls you into his office. You take a seat. Kick off your shoes. Light a cigarette from your hand linked-heel.

Ribbed, stay-up tops. Made by India's leading hosiery-maker to the upper caste. $13. Glowing Charcoal Argyle Socks (No. 555), as described, combustible cotton.

# 20

# I worked for a boss who wanted sex

### By Susan Yount

I had a box knife in my pocket.
I had a tape machine, door card, staple remover.
I had nails that curled under. I had chicken wire in the trunk.
I had dreams we had sex.

I worked for a boss who thought I was smart.

I could use a computer, type, sweep, drink whisky.
I drank black coffee rampantly. I had toenail fungus.
I had bad nail polish. I drank alcohol with coffee.
I had soda sundaes, ran office machines.
I priced all the wheat.

I worked for a boss who thought we were friends.

I had chipped nail polish. I coveted sunglasses.
I suffered from a lack of kindness, hate.
I drank beer mostly. I cleaned office buildings.
I cleaned someone's shit off a toilet lid.
I stole everything.

I temped for a boss I hated.

I had four hours to call a thousand people.
I tried to be good. I could use a computer.
I drank coffee, talked eagerly. I was smart.
I priced health care, had a tape machine.
I left at lunch on my first day.

I worked for a boss who hated me.

I thought he was real cute. I cooked vegetable soup.
I ate grits mostly. I wouldn't obey nor listen nor whatever.
I wore argyle socks and was good at karaoke.
I slipped on butter, fell real hard. I drank whisky.
I found other jobs.

I worked for a boss who paid me to pose.

I rarely wore clothes. I'd lie like tapestry.
I felt each brush stroke. I was on time, cried.
I posed for three hours. I wore a scrap of polyester
If I wore anything. I drank cold coffee. I sneezed.
I ran or walked quickly.

I worked for a boss who liked to watch me work.

I'd lift five pound bundles for twelve hours.
I wore very little. It was hot. I talked a lot. I drank.
I set up machines. I felt my bones, everything.
I had never been so broke. I had never been so wrong.
I took speed. I had a pattern.

I worked for a boss who took me to lunch as reward.

I thought. I noticed. I twisted my hair.
I drank beer, felt smart, used tape.
I could pose. I had benefits. I gained pounds.
I talked business. I priced services. I had manicures.
I wore black shoes.

# 21

# All That It Takes

### By Susan Yount

1.
The lawnmower-switch factory used
tiny springs. Much smaller than any other
spring you have ever seen—of that I am certain,
the circumference of your pupil
staring at sunlit concrete, the length of half
a paperclip—five per switch.
We went through every finger
aligning them as fast as we could.

2.
We beat bundles of labels against tables
until they fanned into plastic (or paper) rainbows—
Tide, Dynamo, Wisk, Snuggle…
Linda must have taken some amphetamines
with teeth that day because she kept cutting
and shoving labels at the packers.
The music changed to death metal.

It is not that her hair grew fast—long, sweaty strands
snaking through the fan breeze—
but that time really passed too quickly.

3.
The day the handmade lampshade factory closed
the women did their best to wear
their fanciest pair of jeans.
But the men were angry and walked too far ahead.

Their boots filled with sand. Turning to glass—
they became transparent, crackling along Lake Michigan,
fires burned right inside them—hearts like little grenades.

# 22

# For Vicki

**By Andrew Neylon**

It was the year of cleaning bathrooms
and looking at the night sky.

The year of cashiering, transporting defectives,
and Vicki chainsmoking right outside.

I asked myself, the day I saw a man
shove a bottle of detergent in a bag

and hobble out the door
and I didn't speak

and he looked like he needed it,
if I was paying for my sins

from a past life. Two weeks
later, watching my manager

do a black Friday war dance,
a white woman belting out

Indian giver claims and the kid
who got an Xbox for Christmas

shoving past me as his mother shouted
I KNOW YOU AIN'T SPECIAL

Working at Target didn't make
me a better person. Reinforced a

lot of what I believed about Jaylen,
who never cleaned the bathroom

on his shift and was so smooth
with the popcorn girls three

got pregnant. Or Marilyn, really
Marina, who used to laugh

at the Russian jokes they made
whenever she refused Wendy's

and told me once, quietly, she
was really from Estonia.

They all talked shit about Vicki, too,
even though she arranged for us all

to sign a card for Theresa after her
father got hit by a drunk driver.

On long nights, a few cars idling away,
I'd sneak an earbud in and let Marc

Maron break the monotony. 15
minute breaks made just of texting girls

I should have stopped talking to after
college. And didn't. Applesauce every

afternoon and clicking through tests
about cleaning up radioactive material.

Unloading boxes of defective material,
wondering if America is leaking

batteries, tainted cans of pineapple,
a busted Fisher-Price™ collection.

From my little hole in the universe the dusky
Indiana sky sometimes seemed to yawn

forever just before it changed to total
darkness and, I guess, the way the moon

reflected off the box-cutter I carried
with me to the far-side of the parking

lot. Yeah, by Macy's,
which didn't seem

so comical a few months after I quit
and two people got shot there.

Hardly seemed like a joke when
the nightly news lady stood in the

icy parking lot and announced
it wasn't even fucking random, just

the long-way-round of some dispute
punctuating our purchases.

Let me tell you the last story,
the one only me and Vicki know.

On my last day, after I tell her I'm
leaving to go hike for seven months

in the mountains, after all of the
managers laugh at me and tell me

I'm too crazy for this or any job,
Vicki hands me a card with my money.

It says, "I just want you know you were
The best at what you did here."

In that moment I realize why I have been
cleaning these toilets, spending my lunch

breaks counting the seconds, listening to
single mothers brag about their children.

# The Contributors

### Cathleen Allyn Conway

Cathleen Allyn Conway is a journalist and inner-city teacher finishing her PhD in creative writing at Goldsmiths College, University of London. She is the co-editor of *Plath Profiles,* the only academic journal dedicated to the work of Sylvia Plath, and the founder and editor of *Thank You For Swallowing.* Her work has appeared in *Bitch, The Mary Sue, 3:AM Magazine, Magma, South Bank Poetry, Ink Sweat and Tears, London Grip, Well Versed* and in anthologies. Her pamphlet *Static Cling* was published by Dancing Girl Press in 2012. Originally from Chicago, she lives in London with her partner and son.

### Vickie Fang

Vickie Fang lives in Maryland with her climate scientist husband and with her hardcore musician son when he's not on tour. She writes full time now instead of practicing law and has recently published historical fiction (*The First of Master Yo's Grand Adventures*) in the Bellevue Literary Review.

### James Figy

James Figy is a writer from Indianapolis and MFA candidate at Minnesota State University, Mankato. He lives with two cats, two rabbits, and one wife, Stephanie, who patiently serves as editor, audience, and champion of his work. He's exceedingly thankful for it. He has a bachelor's degree from the University of Indianapolis and an amateurish collection of Duke Ellington LPs. His creative work has appeared in *Midwestern Gothic, Punchnel's,* and *Flying Island,* among others.

### Alyssa Hubbard

Alyssa Hubbard is an American short story writer and poet from a small town in Alabama. She is a student at the University of Alabama where she is currently obtaining her Bachelor of Arts in English and Creative Writing. Her poetry has been featured in literary magazines and journals such as *Crack the Spine, scissors & spackle,* and the *Marr's Field Journal.* She is currently employed by a large southeastern department store chain and has developed the ability to sense BS over one hundred feet away.

### Chris Huntington

Chris Huntington spent ten years working in Indiana prisons, but currently teaches in Singapore. His first novel, *Mike Tyson Slept Here*, won the 2009 Fabri Literary Prize. His essays on race and family have been featured in *The New York Times,* National Public Radio, and elsewhere. He has an MFA from Bennington College. More information can be found at chrishuntingtononline.com.

### Nate Logan

Nate Logan is from Indianapolis, Indiana. He is the author of three chapbooks, including *Arby's Combo Roundup* (Mondo Bummer, 2010). His work has appeared in a variety of journals including *BOAAT*, *Forklift, Ohio*, and *Ninth Letter*. He is editor and publisher of Spooky Girlfriend Press.

### Tracy Lynn

Tracy Lynn is a writer, blogger, nomad and quasi-adult with a wanderlust that regularly zeroes out her bank account. If you enjoy made up statistics you should check out her blog at *forarainyday.me.*

### Carlo Matos

Carlo Matos has published eight books of poetry, fiction, creative nonfiction and scholarship, including *It's Best Not to Interrupt Her Experiments* (Negative Capability Press) and *The Secret Correspondence of Loon & Fiasco* (Mayapple Press). He has published in many journals including *Boston Review*, *Iowa Review*, and *Another Chicago Magazine*. Carlo has also received grants from the Illinois Arts Council, the Fundação Luso-Americana, and the Sundress Academy for the Arts. He teaches writing at the City Colleges of Chicago and is a teaching artist at the Poetry Barn. After hours he can be found writing poems on demand with Poems While You Wait and practicing the art of the Italian rapier.

### Nancy Matson

Nancy Matson has held over sixty jobs and has had essays published in *Weber: The Contemporary West, Eclectica, Narrative.ly,* and *Gulf Stream Literary Magazine.* She also maintains an environmental blog, Stuff You Don't Want, about how to keep your stuff out of the landfill, item by item, and is a regular contributor to Krrb, where she espouses the virtues of used goods.

## Madeline McEwen

Madeline McEwen is an ex-pat from the UK, bi-focaled and technically challenged. She and her Significant Other manage their four offspring, one major and three minors, two autistic, two neurotypical, plus a time-share with Alzheimer's. You can find her work at her website http://www.madelinemcewen.com.

## Matt Mullins

Matt Mullins writes screenplays, poetry and fiction, and makes filmpoems and digital/interactive literature. His work has been screened at conferences and film festivals in the U.S. and abroad including Zebra, Video Bardo, Visible Verse, FilmPoem, Ó Bhéal, Liberated Words, Co-Kisser and The Body Electric. His fiction and poetry have appeared in a number of print and online literary journals such as *Mid American Review*, *Pleiades*, *Hunger Mountain*, *Descant*, and *Hobart*. His debut collection of short stories, *Three Ways of the Saw*, was published by Atticus Books in 2012 and was named a finalist for *Foreword Reviews* Book of the Year. Matt teaches creative writing at Ball State University where he has been an Emerging Media Fellow at the Center for Media Design. You can engage his interactive/digital literary interfaces at lit-digital.com.

## Andrew Neylon

Andrew Neylon spent his youth criss-crossing the eastern U.S. with his itinerant folks. Neylon recently graduated magna cum laude from Ball State University with a Bachelor's degree in English Literature. In 2011, Neylon co-authored *The Middletown Theatre Project*, about the history of Muncie, Indiana and in 2014 co-authored *If You Don't Outdie Me*, a historical musical about the work of photographer Frank Hohenberger. Additional honors included work with the Invictus Writers and the Kurt Vonnegut Memorial Library in Indianapolis. Neylon's work on the filmic legacy of Hoosier Kurt Vonnegut was presented internationally around Germany during Spring 2014. A four-year team member and two-year co-captain of the BSU Speech Team, Neylon won four national championships in various Individual Events and was honored as the best collegiate forensics speaker in the nation at the 2014 National Forensics Association tournament. Neylon is now involved in the world of television and film production, including recent work with Comcast Spotlight and PBS affiliate WFYI in Indianapolis. In 2015 he completed a 2,189 mile northbound thru-hike of the Appalachian Trail from Georgia to

Maine, and currently lives in Chicago where he works as a speech coach at Northwestern University.

### Noel Osualdini

Noel Osualdini (pronounced Oswald-deeny) spent fifteen years working in call centers after downsizing ended careers in television and government jobs. He lasted a decade in an energy company call center where many staff burned out and left within a few months or years. He is a member of the Australian Horror Writers' Association, and his stories have appeared in various formats in the U.S., U.K. and Australia, as well as in online magazines. He and his partner Joanne live in a menagerie of cats and kids southeast of Melbourne, Australia.

### Elizabeth Philip

Elizabeth Philip resides in the Midwest with her husband, two teenage children, and three dogs. When away from the keyboard, she enjoys reading, cooking, and hiking in the Smoky Mountains. Her experience with a bad job pushed her into early retirement, where she does not have to take any bullshit from anyone.

### Sara Sullivan

Sara Sullivan is the Director of Communications for a U.S. government-funded economic growth development project based in Gaborone, Botswana. After leaving sunny Santa Barbara, she spent twelve years in Washington, D.C. and Boston but still has not fulfilled her dream of someday living in New York City. Sara moved to Islamabad, Pakistan in 2009 as a strategic communications specialist to create awareness campaigns in the country to help dampen anti-American sentiment and communicate the support of the U.S. government to the Pakistani people in agriculture, health, and education programs. She and her husband Drew now live in Botswana, Africa with their two children and yellow Labrador who has been shipped around the world three times now at enormous cost. Sara has a PhD in literature and writes about her time living overseas in Pakistan and Africa at www.outland-ish.com and as a freelance writer for the *Wall Street Journal*. Follow her on twitter @botswanasara.

### Thomas Sullivan

Thomas Sullivan is the author of *Life In The Slow Lane*, a memoir about teaching driver education to teenagers in Oregon. He currently writes short humor essays for the website Humoroutcasts.com. Please visit Thomas at his author website: www.thomassullivanhumor.com.

### Johnny Townsend

Johnny Townsend earned an MFA in fiction writing from Louisiana State University. He has published stories and essays in *Newsday, The Washington Post, The Los Angeles Times, The Humanist, The Progressive, Medical Reform, Christopher Street, The Massachusetts Review, Glimmer Train, Sunstone, Dialogue: A Journal of Mormon Thought,* in the anthologies *Off the Rocks, Queer Fish, In Our Lovely Deseret: Mormon Fictions, Latter-Gay Saints,* and in many other publications. Townsend writes primarily about gay, feminist, and intellectual Mormons, those who don't fit in with traditional Mormon culture. His titles include *Mormon Underwear, Sex among the Saints, Marginal Mormons, Lying for the Lord, Zombies for Jesus,* and *Invasion of the Spirit Snatchers.* He has also written one collection of Jewish short stories, *The Golem of Rabbi Loew,* and one non-fiction book, *Let the Faggots Burn: The UpStairs Lounge Fire.* His collections have been named to Kirkus Reviews' Best of 2011, 2012, 2013, 2014, and 2015. He is also an Associate Producer of the documentary *Upstairs Inferno,* directed by Robert Camina.

### Susan Yount

Susan Yount is the Editor and Publisher of *Arsenic Lobster*; works full-time at the Associated Press; teaches online poetry workshops at the Rooster Moans and is the founder of Misty Publications. In her spare (!) time she moonlights as madam for the Chicago Poetry Bordello. She has two poetry chapbooks, *House on Fire* and *Catastrophe Theory*.

# About The Geeky Press

The Geeky Press is as much a philosophy as it is an entity.

Brad King launched this little group on April 3, 2014 in hopes of building a vibrant writing community in greater downtown Indianapolis. What he didn't have was much of a plan to make that happen. He launched the website, planned a reading series called The Downtown Writers Jam, and hoped that people would come.

And show up they did. Before long, The Geeky Press grew to include more than 100 writers who participated in writing meetups, retreats, reading series, and other literary gatherings.

Before long, The Geeky Press added two amazing partners: Amber Peckham, who is the wittiest writer of the bunch and who corrals our reading series, and Nicole Mathew, who has turned our weekly #WritersHack events into a welcoming writing community.

While The Geeky Press is generally run by the three of us, we've encouraged participants to create their own writing spaces. Now we have members like Reid Delehanty, who has started hosting his own #WritersHack.

In other words, this labor of love has become everything we'd hoped it would be.

*About Brad*

Brad King is an assistant professor in the Department of Journalism where he runs the Center for Emerging Media Design & Development graduate storytelling program. He earned his Masters in Journalism from the University of California at Berkeley's Graduate School of Journalism in 2000, and worked for *Wired* magazine, Wired.com, and *MIT's Technology Review* as a reporter, editor, and senior producer. He's the co-author of *Dungeons & Dreamers: a story of how computer games became a global culture* (ETC Press, 2014). He has two others in process: *So Far Appalachia: An American Mythology* and *Catch: An Oral History of Life and Baseball*. He serves at the editor for Carnegie Mellon's ETC Press, and he's on the program board for South by Southwest Interactive.

*About Amber*

Amber Peckham earned her B.A. in Creative Writing from DePauw University in 2009 and her M.F.A. in Creative Nonfiction at Northwestern University in 2014.

*About Nicole*

Nicole graduated with a B.A. in English (Writing & Literacy) from IUPUI in 2010. She went back to IUPUI to earn her Masters to teach English, but life took another turn and she wound up becoming a Content Specialist (then later a Project Manager) at eGov Strategies, a small company located in Indianapolis. Between graduation and now, Nicole has been a freelance writer in her spare time, doing a lot of writing for the web.

# About Vouched Books Indy

Vouched Books Indy is a pop-up bookstore that loves small press literature & Indianapolis. We sell books & we host readings & sometimes we write reviews on our website, vouchedbooks.com, or on Facebook, www.facebook.com/vouchedbooks/.

Jessica Dyer is a writer (of oh so many things) living in Central Indiana. She's an associate editor at *The Arsenic Lobster Poetry Journal* and is the author of the chapbook *Uterus Poems*. She runs Vouched Books Indy (Indianapolis) and is made of star stuff.

# Visit The Geeky Press

*www.TheGeekyPress.com*

- Sign up for our weekly #WritersHack events
- Sign up for one of our quarterly one-day writing retreats
- Sign up for our annual weekend writing retreat in November
- Submit to (and come) to one of our reading series
- Listen to our writers podcast

# THE GEEKY PRESS

www.ingramcontent.com/pod-product-compliance
Lightning Source LLC
Chambersburg PA
CBHW051830040426
42447CB00006B/462